James Gurney

Catalogue of the choice collection of works of art

James Gurney

Catalogue of the choice collection of works of art

ISBN/EAN: 9783742868985

Manufactured in Europe, USA, Canada, Australia, Japa

Cover: Foto ©Thomas Meinert / pixelio.de

Manufactured and distributed by brebook publishing software
(www.brebook.com)

James Gurney

Catalogue of the choice collection of works of art

CATALOGUE

OF

THE CHOICE COLLECTION OF

WORKS OF ART,

Mostly of the XVth, XVIth and XVIIth Centuries,

FORMED BY THAT

WELL KNOWN CONNOISSEUR,

THE LATE

JAMES GURNEY, ESQ.:

WHICH *(by Order of the Executors)*

Will be Sold by Auction by

Messrs. CHRISTIE, MANSON & WOODS,

AT THEIR GREAT ROOMS,

8 KING STREET, ST. JAMES'S SQUARE,

On TUESDAY, MARCH 8, 1898,

And Four Following Days,

AT ONE O'CLOCK PRECISELY.

———◆———

May be viewed Saturday and Monday preceding, and Catalogues had, at Messrs. CHRISTIE, MANSON and WOODS' Offices, 8 *King Street, St. James's Square, S.W.* ILLUSTRATED CATALOGUES, PRICE TEN SHILLINGS AND SIXPENCE EACH.

CONDITIONS OF SALE.

——o——

I. THE highest Bidder to be the Buyer; and if any dispute arise between two or more Bidders, the Lot so in dispute shall be immediately put up again and re-sold.

II. **No person to advance less than** 1s.; above **Five Pounds, 5s.; and so on in proportion.**

III. **In the case of Lots upon which** there is a reserve, the Auctioneer **shall have the right to bid on** behalf of the Seller.

IV. The Purchasers to give in their Names and Places of **Abode,** and to pay down 5s. in the Pound, or more, in part of payment, or the whole of the Purchase-Money, *if required*; in default of which, the Lot or Lots so purchased **to be** immediately put up again and re-sold.

V. The Lots **to be** taken away and paid for, whether genuine and authentic or not, with all faults and errors of description, at the Buyer's expense and risk, within Two days from the **Sale;** Messrs. CHRISTIE, MANSON and WOODS not being **responsible** for the correct description, genuineness, or authenticity of, or any fault or defect in, any Lot; and making no warranty whatever.

VI. To prevent inaccuracy in delivery, and inconvenience in the settlement of the Purchases, no Lot can on any account be removed during the time of Sale; and the remainder of the Purchase-Money must absolutely be paid on the delivery.

VII. Upon failure of complying with the above Conditions, the Money deposited in part of payment shall be forfeited; all Lots uncleared **within** the time aforesaid shall be re-sold by public or private Sale, and the deficiency (if any) attending such re-sale shall be **made** good by the Defaulter at this Sale.

CATALOGUE.

First Day's Sale.

On TUESDAY, MARCH 8, 1898,

AT ONE O'CLOCK PRECISELY.

SILVER—*At per Oz.*

1 AN ELIZABETHAN PATTERN SERVICE, chased with interlaced strap-work, shells, laurels, &c., consisting of—

Forty-eight table-forks
Twenty-four table-spoons
Eighteen dessert-spoons
Eighteen dessert-forks
One soup-ladle
Eighteen fish-knives
Fish-server and fork, and
One serving-spoon 385 10

	oz. dwt.

2 TWELVE SHELL AND FIDDLE-PATTERN TEA-SPOONS; a pair of sugar-tongs; a mustard-spoon; and twelve oyster-forks 26 7

3 A PAIR OF DITTO ASPARAGUS-TONGS; and a cheese-scoop 10 15

4 A SOUP-LADLE, with scroll-top handle, the edge of bowl fluted and escalloped; and two marrow-spoons . 8 18

B 2

		oz.	dwt.
5	A PAIR OF SAUCE-LADLES, with shell bowls and feathered-edge handles—*old Cork sterling hall mark*	3	0
6	A MARROW-SPOON—*temp. Queen Anne*; a ditto—1741; and a pair of short-handled sugar-spoons, with pierced and chased bowls	6	8
7	EIGHT DESSERT-SPOONS, with chased handles, the bowls embossed with fruit	15	4
8	THREE PLAIN TEA-SPOONS; two ditto, with scroll top handles; four ditto salt-spoons, with shell bowls; a pair of small sugar-tongs; a pair of olive-spikes; a tea-infuser; and a Dutch small three-pronged fork .	5	6
9	A LEMON-STRAINER, with open scroll handles . .	3	2
10	A SMALL PLAIN PAP-BOAT, with reeded border . .	2	15
11	A PAIR OF SMALL PLAIN CREAM-EWERS—1731 .	5	14
12	A SMALL FLUTED CREAM-JUG, engraved with a crest and trellis ornament—1735	4	15
13	A SMALL PLAIN OVIFORM TEA-POT AND COVER—1719	12	4
14	A CREAM-JUG, with reeded border and bands of engraved ornament	4	9
15	A CREAM-JUG, embossed with scrolls and flowers, the base formed of vine ornaments—1746 . . .	5	2
16	A PLAIN CREAM-JUG, with shaped base, faceted body—1720	8	13
17	A SMALL CREAM-JUG, formed as a snail shell, chased with foliage and scrolls, on three mask and shell feet, the handle entwined by a serpent . . .	3	1
18	A PLAIN FACETED HELMET-SHAPED CREAM-JUG, on three scroll feet and with escalloped border . .	5	3
19	A CIRCULAR SUGAR-BASIN, on three feet, repoussé with spiral beading and fluted border—*old Dublin* .	5	12
20	A LARGE CREAM-JUG, chased with a band of classical foliage, with gadroon border and round foot . .	13	0

		oz.	*dwt.*
21	A PLAIN BOWL AND COVER, engraved with a coat-of-arms, scroll-shaped borders—1730 . . .	9	0
22	ANOTHER, similar, engraved with a coat-of-arms and strapwork border—1723	13	7
23	A SET OF THREE SQUARE-SHAPED CANISTERS AND COVERS, with gadroon borders, chased with foliage and shield-shaped ornaments—*by Fox* . .	28	3
	In fish-skin case mounted with **pierced silver** *corners and handle*		
24	A PAIR OF SQUARE-SHAPED CANISTERS AND COVERS, scroll feet and corners chased with wave ornaments, the handles formed as flowers	66	14
25	A TEA SERVICE, consisting of tea-pot and cover, hot-water jug, sucrier and cover, milk-jug, **and a pair of** sugar-tongs, entirely embossed and chased with oblong panels of nymphs on a groundwork of **acanthus foliage**, with animals and reptiles, by ARISTIDE BARRÉ	107	0
	In wood case		
26	A PLAIN COFFEE-POT AND COVER, with moulded base and fluted spout—1752	17	8
27	ANOTHER, smaller, with shell ornament beneath the spout—1744	13	10
28	A GLOBULAR TEA-KETTLE AND COVER, with a band of scroll and diapered ornament in flat chasing, and engraved with a shield-of-arms, on stand pierced **and** chased with classical medallion heads—1738 .	57	0
29	A PLAIN OCTAGONAL TEA-KETTLE, on stand with lamp, of Queen Anne design	52	10
30	A PLAIN SAUCEPAN, with moulded edge . . .	9	8
31	AN OBLONG TOASTED-CHEESE DISH, with reeded border, ebony handle	18	14

		oz.	dwt.

50 A PAIR OF SPIRALLY FLUTED BOWLS AND COVERS, the bases chased with spiral leaf ornaments, scroll handles—1771 . . . . . . **57 0**

51 A PAIR OF OVAL BOWLS, on four **feet**, scroll handles, embossed with flowers and scrolls . . . 22 11

52 A SET OF THREE OVAL DISHES, on feet, scroll handles, embossed in eight petal-shaped panels, engraved with a coat-of-arms and date 1838 . . . . 16 8

53 A HOT-WATER JUG AND COVER, embossed with festoons, laurels and rosette ornaments, beaded ornament round the border—1775 . . . . . 24 2

54 A PAIR OF SAUCE-BOATS, with gadroon borders, scroll handles and shell feet, engraved with a wreath of foliage—1773 . . . . 24 15

55 A PAIR OF LARGER DITTO, similar 32 14

56 A SMALL SAUCE-BOAT, richly **chased** with figures, animals, **scrolls**, &c., in high relief, with open scroll handle chased with a cat, on pierced and chased foot 10 8

From Mr. J. Stewart Hodgson's Collection

57 A PAIR OF TREFOIL-SHAPED WAITERS, the borders chased and pierced with masks, vine ornaments, &c., **the** centres engraved with a shield-of-arms—1750 . 27 3

58 A PAIR OF SQUARE-SHAPED SALVERS, with moulded **borders**, engraved in the centres with coat-of-arms, **and with** borders of scrolls, shells and scale ornament in flat chasing—1754 . . . . 33 7

59 A SMALL SQUARE PLAIN WAITER, engraved with a coat-of-arms—1725 . . . . 8 8

60 A LARGER DITTO, with moulded borders—1726 . 11 15

61 A SALVER, similar 32 10

62 AN OBLONG TWO-HANDLED SALVER, with gadroon and shell border, ball feet 109 14

63 ANOTHER, similar 108 9

	oz. dwt.

64 A TANKARD, with two bands of reeded ornaments . 12 3

65 A SET OF SIX CHAMPAGNE GLASSES, spirally fluted
stems, hexafoil cups 26 15
In oak case

66 A SET OF SIX DITTO 25 14
In oak case

67 A SET OF TWELVE FINGER-BOWLS, after the Tresor
d'Heldersheim, chased in the interior with busts and
honeysuckle ornament, modelled by Monti and chased
by Lekonski, who received the 25th prize for them
from the Goldsmith's Company in 1878 . . 141 0
In oak case

68 A PAIR OF TAPER CANDLESTICKS, circular bases embossed with scrolls, the stems formed as figures of
harlequins—1768 . . . . . 63 15

69 A QUEEN ANNE TAPER CANDLESTICK, octagonal base,
with slight fluted ornament—1702 . . . 4 10

70 A PAIR OF QUEEN ANNE PATTERN TAPER CANDLESTICKS,
on octagonal-shaped stems and feet, with mouldings
and reedings—1728 . . . . . 9 4

71 A PAIR OF CANDELABRA, of Queen Anne design, on
octagonal-shaped stem and feet, with branches for
two lights—1726 . . . . . 54 4

72 A SET OF FOUR FLUTED COLUMN TABLE CANDLESTICKS,
with square-shaped bases, of William III. design . 66 9

73 A CASTER, with fluted base, chased with acanthus leaf
ornaments, gadroon border, the top pierced with
vases, &c.—*old Dublin* 11 5

74 A PLAIN TAZZA, with moulded edge, engraved with a
coat-of-arms in the centre—1715 . . . 5 14

75 A WILLIAM AND MARY CIRCULAR TAZZA, with gadroon
border and foot, the centre engraved with a coat-of-
arms—1690 . . . . . . 10 5

oz. dwt.

76 A **SET OF THREE WILLIAM III. PLAIN OCTAGONAL CASTERS**, moulded bases, the covers pierced with interlaced ornaments—1701—*maker's mark L. U.* . 32 12

77 A **LARGE SPIRALLY FLUTED MUFFINEER**, the base chased with foliage—1752 . . . . . 15 2

78 A **CHARLES II. PLAIN TANKARD AND FLAT COVER**— 1669 . . . . 31 11

79 A **WILLIAM III. SMALLER TANKARD AND COVER**— 1695 . . . . 15 0

80 A **WILLIAM AND MARY TANKARD AND FLAT COVER**, the borders embossed and chased with acanthus foliage, the billet formed of interlaced strap design —1688 . . . . 37 0

81 A **CHARLES II. TANKARD AND FLAT COVER**, engraved with a coat-of-arms—1676—*maker's mark J. S. in a monogram.* 30 14

82 A **CHARLES I. PLAIN GOBLET**, on circular foot and stem, moulded borders—1634 . . . . 6 15

83 A **JACOBEAN CHALICE**, with cylindrical-shaped bowl engraved with **band** of interlaced arabesques, on stem with slight knop and round foot—*the cup,* 1610 . . . . 17 14

SILVER-GILT.

84 **EIGHTEEN ELIZABETHAN PATTERN TEA-SPOONS**; and pair of sugar-tongs 23 4

85 **EIGHTEEN ICE-SPOONS**; and two ice-spades, similar . 31 7

86 **FOUR OBLONG DISHES**, the borders pierced in a foliage design, ruby glass liners 21 4

87 A **PAIR OF GRAPE-SCISSORS**; and two pairs of nut-crackers, the handles boldly chased with fruit and foliage 14 10

		oz.	dwt.
88	SIX COFFEE-SPOONS, with fluted leaf-shaped bowls and plain handles	2	5
89	A PAIR OF LEAF-PATTERN SALT-SPOONS, chased in relief	2	14
90	A FLAT-SHAPED EWER, with scroll handles terminating in serpents' heads, and acanthus below the spout, boldly chased with trellis and rosette ornament, and female masks in high relief—by Rundell, Bridge and Rundell	25	15

From the Octavius Morgan Collection

		oz.	dwt.
91	A CREAM-EWER, with incised ground, of classical form, scroll handle, chased with foliage, with a figure of an angel below and two goats on the spout . .	12	7
92	A PAIR OF SMALL TRAYS, with moulded and engraved borders, fitted with cut-glass bowls . .	8	15
93	A PAIR OF PLAIN MUFFIN-DISHES AND COVERS, with foliage borders, engraved with royal coat-of-arms .	30	4

From the Duke of Sussex's Collection

		oz.	dwt.
94	A BUTTER-DISH AND COVER, of cut-glass and silver-gilt, en suite— *all at*		

From the same

		oz.	dwt.
95	AN EGG-STAND, with four egg-cups and spoons, and salt-cellar, en suite	29	0

From the same

		oz.	dwt.
96	A TOAST-RACK, en suite	13	8

From the same

		oz.	dwt.
97	AN OCTAGONAL TEA-POT, chased and embossed with festoons of flowers and scrolls, and engraved with crests in shield-shaped compartments—1716 .	17	14
98	A SMALL PLAIN CREAM-EWER—1731 . . .	5	3
99	A TEA-POT AND COVER, spirally fluted, the spout formed as a monster's head—1756 . . .	22	9

	oz.	*dwt.*

100 A Pair of Spirally Fluted Canisters and Covers, in two divisions, chased with festoons of flowers, shells and scrolls—1756 18   2

101 A Set of Eight Salt-Cellars and Spoons, tripod fluted feet, festoons of laurels and medallions, glass liners 17   15

    In oak case

102 A Circular Rose-Water Tazza, chased with groups of fruit, flowers and amorini in relief, and with a rose in high relief in the centre, from which a figure of Cupid rises by flotation, on chased vase-shaped stem and round foot 19   0

103 A Parcel-Gilt Tankard, embossed and chased with masks and strapwork, inlaid with sixteen gold coins — *weight of the silver* 54 *oz.* 12 *dwt.*

    In oak case

104 A Charles I. Flat-Shaped Porringer and Cover, parcel-gilt, repoussé with large flowers and scroll foliage, and with flat handles chased with acanthus foliage, the cover repoussé with a figure emblematic of Water, and with three ball feet to form a separate bowl 10   17

105 Four Tazze, circular bases embossed and chased with diapered ornament, fluted vase-shaped stems, the dish of glass mounted with strapwork chased with female heads—*all at*

    In oak case

106 Twelve Dessert-Knives and Forks, with specimen jasper, agate, onyx and other handles

    From Lord Hastings' Collection

SILVER—*All at.*

107 A Nutmeg-Grater, in flattened vase-shaped case

108 **A** Shuttle-Shaped Silver Patch-Box, with engraved borders; and a silver pocket nutmeg-grater, similar

109 A Silver Nutmeg-Grater, formed **as a** snail shell; a **pair of** book-clasps, pierced and delicately chased with flowers; **and** a pair of pierced and fluted ditto

110 A Pierced Silver Counter-Box, chased **with** medallion heads of Charles I. and Henrietta Maria, containing thirty-three silver counters engraved with the Kings of England, **the** Royal arms and inscriptions

111 **An** Oval William III. Box, the **lid** finely engraved with a shield-of-arms in widely gadrooned border, the edges decorated with corded lines— *London hall mark,* 1698

112 **A Silver** Needle-Case, pierced and engraved with scroll foliage, containing a pair of small silver-mounted scissors, a knife and bodkin, and with chain for suspension; a bodkin-case, chased with scrolls, and bodkin; and a silver filigree handkerchief holder, with serpent ring and chain attached

113 **A** Persian Silver Hookah Mount, delicately pierced and chased with birds and scrolls

114 **A** Scandinavian Spoon, with large bowl **and short spiral handle** with chased crown-shaped top and loose rings
From the Shandon Collection

115 **A** Dutch Spoon, with scroll handle surmounted by a figure of **an Indian** bearing **a** barrel, engraved with inscription and date 1609
From the Shandon Collection

116 A Dutch Spoon, with spiral handle, partly chased with em-**blematic figures** and surmounted **by** a figure of a workman; **and a small** steel knife, with silver handle, the top pierced **with scrolls**

117 A Dessert-Knife, the handle chased as a figure of a knight in armour

118 A Set of Four **Blue Glass** Sauce-Bottles, mounted **with** silver handles, rims, neck-bands, and corks

119 A Pair of Cluster Column Candlesticks, with masks and festoons of drapery below, beaded ornament round the borders —1772

120 A Set of Six Cups, each formed as **half** an emu's egg, finely mounted with vine foliage, animals and insects in chased silver—*in wood case*

FOREIGN SILVER.

	oz. dwt.

121 A Tea-Pot, hot-water jug, cream-jug, sucrier and cover, and basin, spirally fluted, chased with shell-shaped ornaments of Louis XV. design—*by Odiot, Paris* 62 11
    In wood case

122 An Old Dutch Plain Toy Tea Service, consisting of circular salver **with** threaded border, on scroll feet, tea-pot, tea-urn, sugar-basin and covers, milk-jug and two tea-cups—*Amsterdam* . . . 8 19

123 An Old Dutch Plain Cylindrical Spice-Box, in two divisions, with waved thread band round the centre, **and on** three feet, **the** cover repoussé with flowers **and** foliage, **and** surmounted by a figure of St. Catherine, engraved underneath with inscription **and** date 1712. . . . . . . 8 4

124 A Pair of Single Ditto, on three ball feet, the covers chased with scroll foliage, and surmounted by large vase-shaped ornament, the rims of lids pricked with inscriptions 11 10

125 A Small Old German Goblet, with shallow lobed bowl **and** punched ornament in **centre,** and alternate engraved panels, on stem with **chased** open scroll ornament, and **round** fluted foot 4 2

14

oz. dwt.

126 **A** SMALL OLD GERMAN TANKARD, with flat **cover, finely**
engraved with Scriptural subjects **and arabesques,**
an armed winged **figure** holding **shields on the lid,**
and inscription, **on** three gourd **and tendril feet,**
and with curious pierced triple **fan-shaped orna-**
ment inside the lid, and gilt inside . . . 8 15

127 A SMALL **OLD SWEDISH** PEG TANKARD **AND COVER,**
on three ball feet, with scroll handle and eagle and
serpent billet, the lid engraved with date 1663 . 9 19

128 **A** CIRCULAR FLAT-SHAPED TEA-POT, chased **with shells**
and scroll foliage on scale-pattern ground, and **with**
bird's-head spout—*Rotterdam* 11 10

129 **A** SMALL OVAL DISH, the centre **chased with an** equestrian figure in landscape, the **border repoussé with**
a stag hunt and scroll foliage—*by Jacob Warm-*
burger, Augsburg, circa 1690 . . . . 4 12

130 **A** CIRCULAR ROSE-WATER DISH, with deeply fluted
and escalloped border, the centre repoussé with
foliage and laurel wreath and engraved with scrolls
on seeded ground, and engraved on the outside
with a bust portrait of King Henry VI. of England
—*Portuguese* . : 16 3

131 **A** PAIR OF TABLE CANDLESTICKS, on octagonal bases,
gadrooned and beaded ornaments on the stems—
Regensburg 15 16

132 **A** PAIR OF TABLE CANDLESTICKS, of Louis XV. design,
chased with scrolls, festoons of laurels, &c., **and**
fitted with scroll branches for three **lights** . . 66 10

FOREIGN SILVER-GILT.

oz. dwt.

133 A PAIR OF SHELL-SHAPED TOILET-BOXES AND COVERS, with panels and borders of shell ornament in flat chasing—*by John Conrad Schnell, Augsburg, early 18th century* 5 2

134 A PAIR OF CIRCULAR DITTO, en suite, with pierced flat handles, the covers with three feet to form separate bowls—*by the same* 5 10

135 AN OVAL FLUTED BOWL AND COVER, on foot, chased with panels of flowers, scroll foliage and cherubs— *Dresden, 18th century* 8 15

136 AN OVAL DISH, with spirally fluted border and shaped reeded edge, with border of shell and scroll ornament in flat chasing—*Augsburg* 8 11

137 THE COMPANION DISH, of copper-gilt

138 A PLATE, of copper-gilt, en suite

139 A PLAIN LOUIS XV. CUP, COVER AND TREMBLEUSE STAND, with reeded borders—*Paris* . . . 12 1

140 A SMALL RUSSIAN JUG, with parcel-gilt cover, chased as sewn linen, and engraved with plaited rush-work on the body 3 10

141 A TRAVELLING SERVICE, decorated with shell ornament in flat chasing, and engraved with monogram and crown, consisting of dessert-fork and spoon, knife with steel blade, tea-spoon with marrow-spoon handle, and shell-shaped condiment-box—*Augsburg* —in stamped leather case—*nett weight without knife* 6 14

142 A SILVER-GILT CREAM-JUG, supported by a griffin shell-shaped body, the handle formed as a serpent, chased with masks in low relief—*by Van Vianen* . 8 4
    From the Collection of Octavius Morgan

oz. dwt.

143 A TRIANGULAR SALT-CELLAR, of silver-gilt, the feet
formed as lions upholding shields, egg and tongue
ornaments round the edge, three salt-wells, the
borders engraved with scrolls, &c., the whole surmounted by a Roman warrior—*Augsburg, 16th
century*   4   2

From the Londesborough Collection

144 A PAIR OF CIRCULAR SILVER-GILT SALT-CELLARS,
supported on three cherubs' heads, the borders
engraved with interlaced scrolls—*German, 16th
century*   3   4

145 A DOUBLE DRINKING-CUP, of silver-gilt, formed as
a barrel, the bases engraved with the figures of
St. Michael and St. John—*Nuremburg, 17th century*   6   14

146 A GOBLET, with large bowl, decorated with punched
spiral bands and pricked trellis work, on vase-shaped
stem and round foot, with interlaced strap and other
ornament in flat chasing—*5½ in. high—Augsburg,
maker's mark, circa 1609* .   .   .   6   9

From the Shandon Collection

147 A TALL SLENDER GOBLET, parcel gilt, the bowl of
inverted bell form, engraved with strap and foliage
ornament **and festoons, on** vase-shaped **stem** with
finely modelled knop chased with cherubs and
scrolls in relief, and round foot slightly engraved—
7½ in. high—Berlin, 17th century   .   .   4   16

148 A BEAKER-SHAPED GOBLET, parcel-gilt, the bowl engraved with interlaced pricked strap ornament and
scroll foliage, and finely chased with three horned
monsters' heads in high relief, on flattened knop
chased with scrolls, and round foot chased with
raised lozenge ornament in ribbon borders—*5½ in.
high—Augsburg, 17th century*   .   .   .   5   14

oz. dwt.

149 A **LARGE** TANKARD AND COVER, parcel-gilt, chased
with medallions of children emblematic of the
Seasons, in borders **of** arabesque foliage and scrolls
in appliqué work, the borders decorated with flat
chasing, and engraved inside the lid with shields-
of-arms and date 1727—*by Johann Philipp Höfler,
Nuremburg* **32** 15

150 A SILVER-GILT STANDING CUP AND COVER, circular
base, depressed knob, cylindrical cup, the cover surmounted by a small classical figure, the whole
embossed and chased with interlaced strapwork,
masks, fruit, &c.—*Augsburg, late 16th century* . 7 14

End of First Day's Sale.

Second Day's Sale.

On WEDNESDAY, MARCH 9, 1898,

AT ONE O'CLOCK PRECISELY.

CARVINGS IN IVORY.

151 A LOUIS XIV. NEEDLE CASE, carved in low relief with arabesques and scroll ornament, mounted with metal-gilt

152 A SET OF THREE KNIVES AND THREE FORKS, the handles of ivory finely carved with groups of dogs attacking wild animals, silver blades—*late 17th century*

> *Exhibited at the Art Treasures Exhibition, Manchester, 1857, and at Leeds, 1868*
>
> *From the Shardon Collection*

153 THE HILT OF A HUNTING SWORD, the grip carved as a group of the Sacrifice of Iphigenia, diagonally curved quillons and single knuckle ring carved with the same subject, terminating in arabesques—*17th century*—6 *in. high,* 5¼ *in. wide*—on carved ebonised stand

> *Vide Illustration*

154 THE LID OF A SNUFF-BOX, carved in high relief with Venus attended by Cupids, Flora, Pomona, Pan and other deities, presenting flowers, fruit, &c., the reverse painted with a river scene and figures, in oils, by Ferg

> *Vide Illustration*

155 AN OLD ENGLISH IVORY FAN, very finely pierced and carved
with medallion of flowers in the centre, circular medallions
on either side with trophies, the mount of Honiton lace with
bouquets of flowers, butterflies and insects

156 THE HILT OF A HUNTING SWORD, the pommel and grip carved
as a terminal mailed figure and crouching lion, scale-pattern
quillons terminating in leopards' heads and trophies of arms
and masks in the centre—*circa* 1700—5½ *in. high,* 4 *in. wide*

157 A LOUIS XIV. RAPOIR, carved in low relief with Venus seated
on clouds, with doves, floriated foliage above and below,
terminating in shell—8¼ *in. long*
Vide Illustration

158 ANOTHER, carved in low relief, with Venus and Cupid, fluted
columns on either side, and canopies above and arabesque
ornament below, with pierced iron grater at back—9¼ *in. long*
Vide Illustration

159 TWO BOYS AT PLAY: a carving in high relief, by FIAMINGO,
arched top—4½ *in.* by 3 *in.*—in ebony frame
From General Buller's Collection

160 A CIRCULAR SNUFF-BOX, carved in low relief with Hercules and
the Cretan Bull in shaped panel in the centre, and hunting
subjects, &c.—*temp* Louis XV.
Vide Illustration

161 FRAGMENT OF A DIPTYCH, carved in high relief with The
Flagellation—14*th century*

162 A TRIPTYCH, the centre panel divided into three flamboyant
Gothic canopies, the centre one carved with the Virgin and
Child, St. Catherine and St. John, on either side are St. Peter
and St. Paul, the emblems of the Evangelists in each corner,
the wings carved with four subjects from the Life of Christ
—5 *in. high, opening* 8½ *in wide*—*French Gothic,* 15*th century*
From the Shandon Collection
Vide Illustration

163 A PAIR OF SIDES OF A SHUTTLE, finely pierced and carved with
a shepherd, shepherdess, sheep, gardening and musical
trophies on a scroll-pattern ground—*French, 18th century*

164 A SMALL CARYATID FEMALE BUST, carved with scroll ornaments at the sides and festoons of flowers—*circa* 1640

165 THE GRIP OF A HUNTING SWORD, boldly carved with a **boar**-
hunting subject, mounted with gold ferrule and tiddle—
French, 18th century

166 AN UPRIGHT PLAQUE, carved in relief with a knight and lion, the
knight wears a cylindrical helmet, mail brassards and jambes,
and long surcoat, and is armed with a short braquemart and
small triangular shield—*13th century*—3 *in.* by 2¼ *in.*

   From the Shandon Collection
   Vide Illustration

167 A GROUP, of the Virgin carrying the Infant Saviour and holding
a rose, standing on the serpent—5½ *in. high—on socle—*
Flemish, 17th century

168 THE HILT OF A STILETTO, carved as a group of Venus and Cupid,
the quillons terminating in spiral curls—*English, circa* 1590

169 A CYLINDRICAL NEEDLE-CASE, delicately engraved with a spiral
band of an equestrian battle subject, a narrow band above
and below engraved with shields-of-arms and amorini bearing
crowns—*inscribed* Bartolomeo Sforeza, *faciebat* 1584

170 A PAIR OF KNIFE-HANDLES, finely carved, one with a lion and
hounds, the other with a bear, boar, wolf and hounds in
relief—*17th century*

   Exhibited at the Art Treasures Exhibition, Manchester, 1857
   From the Shandon Collection

171 A MEMENTO MORI, showing on the one side the decayed flesh
with a lizard and toad, and on the other the skull, and through
the cheek bone is coiled a snake—*17th century—by Christopher
Harrich*

   From the Shandon Collection
   Vide Illustration

172 A HAND MIRROR, in octagonal-shaped ivory case, with a shield-
shaped panel in the centre delicately carved with an equestrian
encounter, and on each side two seated figures of Roman
captives, below in upright cartouche is the figure of Victory,
figures and festoons of fruit on either side, the handle formed
as a column—*signed* B. Pittoni, 1583

GOLD COINS.

173 RICHARD II. NOBLE, without flag, and with French and Aquitaine titles, *rev.* usual type, B. in the centre of *rev.—very fine*   1

174 **HENRY** VI. QUARTER NOBLE, with lis over shield, mullet after EXALTABITVR, and annulet after IN, **m.m.** lis—*very fine*   1

175 EDWARD VI. SOVEREIGN, sixth year, m.m. Y, half-length **figure of** the king, crowned and in armour, holding sword **and orb,** *rev.* Royal Arms with supporters, below E·R **on a scroll—*very fine and rare***   1

176 GEORGE IV. FIVE-POUND PIECE, 1826—*brilliant*   1

177 GEORGE **IV. Two-POUND PIECE—** *extremely fine*   1

178 GEORGE **IV. SOVEREIGN and** HALF-SOVEREIGN—*very fine*   2

179 ELIZABETH FINE SOVEREIGN (*Rud.* ix. 8), m.m. tun, Queen robed and seated in a regal chair with ornamental back, and portcullis at her feet, *rev.* usual legend and type—*very fine*   1

180 ELIZABETH HALF-SOVEREIGN (*Rud.* x.), m.m. woolpack, bust with high crown and long hair over shoulders, usual legends and types—*extremely fine*
    From the Johnson and Brice Collections   1

181 ELIZABETH MILLED HALF-SOVEREIGN (*Rud.* x. **7), broader bust** with grained edge—*very fine and rare*   1

182 JAMES I. THIRTY-SHILLING PIECE, **variety** of *Rud.* XII. **5, m.m.** trefoil, king upon throne, with plain back, with his feet on a portcullis, *rev.* A·DNO, &c., shield-of-arms surmounted by XXX. **within** a circle of lis, lions and **roses—*extremely fine,*** *and a rare variety*   1

183 JAMES I. LAUREL, m.m. spur rowel, of fine work, with the larger shield on *rev.—very fine*   1

184 CHARLES II. FIVE-GUINEAS, 1671, Vicesimo Tertio, small bust, with lovelock—*extremely fine, a date unknown to Kenyon*   1
    From the Bieber Collection

185 JAMES II. HALF-GUINEA, 1688—*very fine*   1

186 ANNE HALF-GUINEA BEFORE UNION, 1705, with rose in centre—
    brilliant   1
        From the Bieber Collection

187 GEORGE III. PATTERN SEVEN-SHILLING PIECE, by Yeo, bust to
    right, *rev.* lion on crown, 1776, edge plain—*brilliant and*
    scarce   1

ECCLESIASTICAL METAL WORK.

188 A BRONZE TAPER-STAND, with pierced bulb nozzle, the foot
    chased with three grotesque figures of animals in relief—*14th*
    century
        From the Magniac Collection

189 A COPPER-GILT PYX, with pointed cover surmounted by a
    circular knob, engraved with annular rosette ornaments—*14th*
    century—3 *in. high*

190 A RELIQUAIRE, of copper-gilt, shaped as an arm with outstretched
    palm, loose sleeve set with three jewels at the wrist, an
    upright opening in the centre of the forearm for the display
    of relics—*14th century*—10 *in. high*
        From the Bateman Collection

191 A PEAR-SHAPED ALTAR-BOTTLE, of copper-gilt, embossed and
    chased with an oval medallion on either side, decorated with
    " The Flagellation," laurel foliage borders, cherubs' heads
    above and below on a spirited groundwork of acanthus
    leaves and scrolls—*Italian, circa* 1600
        From the His de la Salle Collection

192 A RELIQUARY, copper-gilt, the base formed as three figures of
    dragons, the body shaped as a cylindrical tower pierced with
    Gothic tracery windows, leaning buttresses and circular spire,
    surmounted by a cross—13*th century*—10½ *in. high*
        From the Bernal Collection, No. 1300
        From the Bateman Collection
        Vide Illustration

193 A SMALL COPPER-GILT **CASE**, shaped as a book, engraved on **the** one side with a figure of Mars in Romanesque armour, on **the** corresponding side Venus holding an **arrow** and flaming **heart**, the inside containing two **small oval** portraits **of Saints**, in oils—*middle of 16th century*

194 A CHALICE AND COVER, of copper-gilt, octagonal faceted base with **a slight** beaded ornament, cylindrical stem, depressed knop, **shallow** bowl and cover hinged in two places, and surmounted by **a** crucifix with saints on either side—*Flemish*, *15th century*

> *From the Bateman Collection*
> *Vide Illustration*

195 A PIERCED COPPER-GILT CENSER, engraved with conventional foliage, the cover surmounted by two tiers of Gothic canopies and pinnacles, engraved with herring-bone ornaments, suspension chains and rosette loop—*Flemish, 15th century*

> *From the Bateman Collection*
> *Vide Illustration*

196 A PROCESSIONAL CRUCIFIX, of copper-gilt, **the** ends of the cross terminating in circular discs representing the Evangelists, **plaited borders, and** engraved with geometrical ornament; on **either side are movable** branches with statuettes of Joseph and **Mary—15th** century—$19\frac{1}{2}$ in. **by** 13 in.

> *From the Bateman Collection*

197 A BOAT-SHAPED INCENSE VESSEL, OR **"NAVETTE,"** in gilt copper —*Italian work, circa* 1460—10 in. long, extreme height $4\frac{1}{2}$ in.

The triangular compartments formed by the lids are each beautifully engraved, one with a half-figure of St. Catherine within a cusped ogee-shaped quatrefoil, and the other that of a bishop with a nimbus. The ground space around the quatrefoils is engraved with foliage, and at each extremity of the vessel, perched on the apex or prow, is a small figure of a winged dragon, one of which serves as a handle to open the movable lid. A most beautiful specimen, probably of North Italian work. The use of this vessel was to contain the incense burnt during the service of the altar; the ancient spoon with which the incense was put into the thurible is preserved with the present specimen.

H. M

> *The plaque in the interior probably represents the successor to the Bishop on the top, over whose portrait it was affixed with gum mastic when purchased at the Magniac Collection*
> *From the Magniac Collection*
> *Vide Illustration*

LOCKS AND KEYS.

198 A STEEL KEY, with pierced and beaded bow, fluted barrel—
4½ in. long—17th century
From the Shandon Collection

199 A STEEL KEY, the bow finely pierced with monogram and
scrolls, fluted and beaded barrel—5¾ in. long
From the same Collection
Vide Illustration

200 A SMALLER KEY, the bow pierced and chased with acanthus
foliage surmounted **by** a crown, quatrefoil barrel engraved
with acanthus foliage—3¼ in. long—17th century
From the same Collection

201 A STEEL KEY, *temp* Louis XV., the bow pierced and shaped with
scroll and leaf ornaments, double spiral barrel surmounted
by a chased capital—6 in. long
Vide Illustration

202 A KEY, of blued steel, with curiously shaped and pierced bow,
fluted square-shaped barrel engraved with incised lines—
4¾ in. long—early 17th century
Vide Illustration

203 A KEY, with pierced and shaped bow, surmounted by seven small
rosette ornaments, spirally fluted barrel—5½ in. long—17th
century
Vide Illustration

204 A KEY, with circular pierced bow, fluted barrel—4½ in. long—
17th century; and a key, with pierced trefoil-shaped bow—
3½ in. long—18th century

205 A KEY, of blued steel, the bow pierced and chased, surmounted
by a ducal coronet, quatrefoil-shaped barrel—4 in. long—
middle of 17th century
From the Shandon Collection
Vide Illustration

206 A KEY, with finely chased bow pierced with interlaced cipher
L.L., quatrefoil-shaped barrel—3¾ in. long—17th century
Vide Illustration

207 Two STEEL KEYS, with pierced and floriated bows and fluted
barrels—18th century

208 A KEY, *temp* Louis XVI., the bow chased with festoons of laurel
and architectural ornament—3½ in. long

209 A STEEL KEY, the **bow** finely pierced with cipher and floriated
ornament, the barrel pierced with acanthus leaves—5½ *in. long*
—17th century
From the Shandon Collection
Vide Illustration

210 AN IRON KEY, with open bow shaped as a thistle, cross-hatched
stem and large elaborate wards—6 *in. long*—15th century
From Holyrood Palace
From the Shandon Collection
Vide Illustration

211 A SMALL KEY, of somewhat similar form—2½ *in. long*
From the same

212 A STEEL KEY, the **bow** pierced and chiselled with two **dragons**
supporting a crown, fluted, beaded and pierced barrel, **and**
fluted wards—4½ *in. long*—17th century
From the Shandon *Collection*
Vide Illustration

213 AN ENGRAVED METAL-GILT KEY, with **pierced** floriated bow and
monogram G. R., surmounted **by a** Royal crown, fluted barrel
engraved with acanthus leaves—5½ **in.** *long*—18th century
From the Shandon Collection
Vide Illustration

214 A LARGE STEEL KEY, the bow pierced with quatrefoil ornament,
fluted trefoil-shaped barrel surmounted by an annular ornament—8 *in. long*—16th century
From the Shandon Collection

215 A STEEL KEY, with pierced floriated **bow** surmounted **by a**
coronet, fluted barrel engraved **with** acanthus leaves—4½ **in.**
long—end of 17th century
From the Shandon Collection
Vide Illustration

216 A STEEL KEY, the **bow** pierced and chased with reversed cipher
C. enclosing VI. **in** Roman numerals, surmounted by a crown
supported by dragons (Charles VI. of Sweden), fluted barrel
and open ward—5 **in.** *long*
From the Shandon Collection
Vide Illustration

217 A STEEL-GILT KEY, with quatrefoil-shaped bow chased **with**
initials R. R., surmounted by a crown and pierced borders,
the barrel and wards chased with acanthus leaves—5½ *in.*
long, signed—early 17th century
From the Shandon Collection
Vide *Illustration*

218 A Steel Key, with pierced floriated bow surmounted by a Royal crown, fluted barrel and ward—4½ in. long—late 17th century

From the Shandon Collection

Vide Illustration

219 A Steel Key, with pierced and chiselled arabesque bow, fluted and beaded barrel of quartrefoil shape—4¼ in. long—17th century

From the Shandon Collection

Vide Illustration

220 A Gilt Metal Lock, with seated figures of hounds, scrolls, shell ornament in low relief, the bolt formed as a seated bloodhound—*temp* Louis XIV.

221 A Lock, with steel plate overlaid with appliqué scrolls **and** floral ornaments in brass—*temp* Louis XV.

From the Shandon Collection

222 A Lock, painted in the Chinese taste, double scroll handles and pierced key

223 A Lock and Key, of bright steel of intricate design, curious pierced Gothic borders, dome-shaped centre supported by pierced columns, containing a coat-of-arms with palm-leaf borders, the key of square pilaster form, chiselled with masks in relief—*late 17th century*

From the Shandon Collection

224 A **Lock, of** bright steel, in oblong roped border containing three panels of interlaced Gothic tracery, the handle of the bolt forms a grotesque head—*early 16th century*

From the Shandon Collection

225 A Lock and Key, the case of brass finely pierced with a grotesque mask and virated scrolls, vandyked ornaments at the sides engraved with scrolls, annular ground, beaded borders; the lock of blued steel; the barrel and ward piercing formed as trefoil ornaments; the key of bright steel, elaborately interlaced scroll bow, quartrefoil-shaped barrel with turned ornament below the bow, slightly engraved with acanthus leaves—3½ in. by 3½ in.—*middle of the 17th century*

From the Hume Campbell Collection

*From the **Bernal** Collection*

226 A Lock and Key, of **bright** steel, the front plate of the **lock**
enclosed in a finely moulded border, in **the** centre of which
is a panel of architectural design, supported on either **side**
by fluted Doric columns; by touching the spring in the
centre of the left-hand capital the front falls, disclosing
the key-hole; the front finely chased and chiselled in high
relief with a coat-of-arms supported **on either** side by
rampant lions, and surmounted by a **crown; two** cornucopiæ
on the architrave; on either side of the **centre are two pierced**
scroll panels of oak and laurel branches, **the one on the**
right opens by **touching** the spring in **the right capital,**
the back opening disclosing a lock of the finest workmanship;
the key of curious form, chiselled and minutely pierced **with**
intricate interlaced design—*English, circa* 1690

    From the Shandon Collection
    Vide Illustration

227 A KEY, of **bright steel, the** bow **very** finely chased and
pierced; in **the centre** a thistle-shaped panel bearing an
interlaced cipher surmounted by a ducal crown; gilt background, richly beaded and scrolled border; the barrel pierced
and turned with beaded acanthus leaf and crown ornaments;
the ward **engraved in** alternate bands with acanthus leaves,
terminating in a fruit-shaped knob—*late 17th century*

    From the William Meyrick Collection
    Vide Illustration

228 THE STAR CHAMBER LOCK AND KEY OF KING
CHARLES II., formerly the **property** of the Duke **of**
Ormond; **the works** of the lock **are of** steel overlaid with
plates of brass, and decorated with finely cut appliqué orna-
mentation and band of leaf and **thistle** engraving, the three
handles formed as chased rosettes; **the key** of steel, elaborately
chiselled, pierced and chased with two portraits of Charles II.
in armour, wearing a wig and ruff, on a gilt background in a
border of floral scrolls and beading, **the** stem formed as a
pierced and turned column

    Vide Illustration

ORIENTAL ARMS.

228ᴀ A Back Scratcher, in silver and gilt **metal** turned haft, **con**-
taining a stiletto with circular blade

229 An Indian **Nagwatch** or Tiger's Claw, of russet steel, damascened with **scrolls** and ornaments in gold; each of the five
blades **is fitted with a** small silver-mounted sheath

230 An **Indian Sikh** Knife, the grip overlaid with plaques **of
horn, and** secured by five rivets with pearl heads mounted
in gold; the blade finely damascened, chiselled and chased
at the back, and running up the tang with spirited floral ornaments partly damascened in gold—13 *in. long*; the sheath
in velvet, mounted with pierced and chased silver chains for
suspension

231 Collection Spitzer, *numerous plates, some coloured*, 6 vol. *royal
folio, half-bound red morocco extra, uncut, top edge gilt*

Paris, 1890-92

ARMS AND ARMOUR.

232 A Skiendhu, the grip of ebony carved with interlaced cord
work, mounted with silver chased with thistles, and mounted
with cairngorm; the blade—4½ *in. long*—back-edged and
serrated, leather scabbard mounted in silver

233 A Delicate Pear-Shaped Powder-Primer, of russet iron, inlaid with scrolls, birds and panels, bead border—*17th century*

234 A Flat Pear-Shaped Powder-Primer, of russet iron, with
shaped panel in the centre with figures of ladies and gentlemen, scrolls and fleur-de-lis ornament inlaid in silver—*17th
century*

235 A Gun-Stock Mount, of bright steel, chiselled and chased in low relief with grotesque masks and interlaced arabesques; a pair of pistol-stock mounts, chased with trophies of armour; and two other pieces, with grotesque masks and scrolls in low relief—*late 17th century*   5

236 A Small Steel Model of a Stirrup, chased with scrolls and rosette; and a blued steel gun-sight   2

From the Greenwood Collection

237 A Small Halberd-Head, of bright steel, flamboyant four-sighted spike, double drooping beak, and open crescent-shaped axe-blade—*17th century*

From the Greenwood Collection

238 A Dagger, the grip octagonal in section, of silver, inlaid with laurel patterns in gold, steel laurel-pattern cap pommel; the blade —10½ *in. long*—finely grooved, moulded and pierced in the centre with a serpent, above a sword and laurel leaf crossed, encircled by a snake, the emblem of Eternity— *Spanish, late 18th century*

239 A Dagger, ivory grip, the mounts of russet iron damascened in gold, by Ronzon; the blade—6 *in. long*—similarly orna-mented, mounted sheath

240 A Short Curved Sword, entirely mounted with bronze-gilt, floriated pommel and curved leaf quillons, chased in low relief with interlaced arabesque ornament; the blade—11½ *in. long* —slightly curved and back-edged, the grip of ivory engraved and inlaid with an interlaced design, the scabbard of copper-gilt, similarly ornamented to the hilt—*Venetian, 16th century*

From the Sasson Collection

241 A RAPIER, the **hilt of** gilt steel, oviform pommel, curved quillons, knuckle bow, single bars and large shells; the **ends** of the quillons, end and centre of the knuckle guard **and** single ring chiselled as a turbaned negro's head; the ground-work inlaid with scrolls, dotted ornaments and **rosettes in** silver on a gold ground; the shells pierced in two **diamond-**shaped panels with diaper ornaments on a scale-pattern ground; the blade—44 *in. long*—six-sided, grooved and inscribed MONTE ✠ ENN ✠ TOLEDO—*circa* 1600

242 A SHELL-HILTED RAPIER, of bright steel, with depressed pommel decorated in two panels with flowering **scrolls**; long straight quillons and knuckle bow, terminating in turned ends; the shell is finely chased and pierced on either side with birds, dolphins, interlaced lilies, and bordered by bands **of** laurel ornaments; the inner shell similarly ornamented—the two shells joined by bars of five rings; the whole of **the hilt** with the exception of the pommel is forged out of one **piece;** blade—41 *in. long*—curiously back-edged, and grooved **on the** defensive side, slightly engraved with monsters and **scrolls,** the armourer's mark on the ricasso—*Spanish, circa* 1615
From the Meyrick collection

243 A STILETTO, entirely of bright steel, the grip composed of monkeys one above the other, the quillons formed as dolphins; **the** blade—7 *in. long*—triangular—17*th* **century.** *Brescian*

244 A STILETTO, entirely **of** bright steel, oviform pommel, ends to the quillons, the grip spirally fluted; the blade—7½ *in. long* —four-sided and grooved, said to be for poison—17*th* century
Exhibited at the New Gallery, Early Italian Art, 1894

245 A STAG'S HORN POWDER FLASK, engraved with annular and zigzag ornaments, small primer and measure attached, studded leather belt—*Swedish,* 17*th century*
From the Shandon Collection

246 A POWDER FLASK AND SPANNER, carved **in low** relief with figures in **the** last century costume

247 A BANNER HEAD, of bright steel, finely chiselled and moulded as a fleur de lis, taken at the Battle of St. Quintin, August 10th, 1557

From the Shandon Collection

248 A DAGGER, the hilt of steel, chiselled as a Romanesque warrior armed with oval shield and falchion, partly blued and plated with silver, and standing on the capital of a Corinthian column; the blade—7 *in. long*—back-edged within two inches of **the hilt, alight** ricasso engraved with scrolls **and** date 1582, and gilt, the armourer's mark inlaid in copper

From the Londesborough Collection

249 A RAPIER, with swept hilt of bright steel, faceted oviform pommel with four oval panels in relief; knuckle guard, straight quillons and triple bar, the lowest one containing small shells; the ends of the quillons, the end and **centre of** the knuckle guard and centres of the ring formed as spirally fluted lobes; the bars, quillons, &c., entirely decorated with reverse cut ornament; the blade—44 *in. long*—six-sided and doubly grooved, strong ricasso—*circa* 1600

From the Meyrick Collection
Illustrated in Skelton

250 A RAPIER, the hilt of russet iron, fluted, and roped barrel-shaped pommel, knuckle bow, straight quillons slightly swelling at the ends, triple ring and large pas d'âne; the whole of the hilt inlaid with virated scrolls in silver, plaited wire grip; the blade—44 *in. long*—four-sided, inscribed on the ricasso—*Antonio Picino*—*circa* 1600

251 A PRESENTOIR, OR SERVING-KNIFE— *German work, circa* 1570—15½ *in. long*

The hilt is in massive gilt copper, exquisitely chiselled with trap-work ornament, terminal figures, cornucopiæ, &c., and inlaid on each side with two small panels of minute chequered mosaic of ivory and dark-coloured wood.

H. M.

From the Magniac Collection
Vide Illustration

252 A POMMEL, of bright steel, chiselled and pierced with five small canopies, supported by terminal figures and festoons **of** drapery, grotesque masks above—*Italian, circa* 1620

> *From the Shandon Collection*

253 A PAIR OF MILITARY SHEARS, of **bright steel, engraved with** trophies **of** Romanesque armour, **griffins, &c., in fluted open-** work steel scabbard—*circa* 1560

> *Engraved in Skelton*
> *From the Meyrick Collection*

254 A LEFT-HAND DAGGER, the hilt **of** russet steel minutely damascened with interlaced scrolls in gold, octagonal pommel, square-shaped quillons broadening at the ends and drooping strongly towards the blade, single knuckle ring; the blade—10 *in. long*—stiff and four-sided, strong ricasso similarly ornamented to the hilt

> *Exhibited at the New Gallery Early Italian Art,* 1894

255 A STILETTO, the hilt entirely of bright steel, in eight parts, cut with jewelled ornaments; the blade—7½ *in. long*—stiff and four-sided, in leather scabbard, in bright steel mounts of similar design

256 **A DAGGER,** the hilt **of bright** steel, fluted pommel, straight fluted quillons **and single ring,** copper wire grip; the blade—6¾ *in. long*—six times grooved, pierced serrated edge, and terminating in an arrow point

> *From the Meyrick* **Collection**
> *Illustrated in Skelton*
> *Exhibited at the New Gallery Early Italian Art,* **1894**

257 A STILETTO, of bright steel, turned pommel, grip and quillons, drooping shell guard engraved with grotesque monster; **the** blade—7¼ *in. long*—formed as **a** pistol barrel—*17th century*

> *From the Shandon Collection*
> *Exhibited at the New Gallery Early Italian Art,* 1894

258 A STILETTO, entirely of steel, the pommel formed as a helmeted head, reversed dolphin grip and quillons ending in floriated knobs; the blade—6½ *in. long*—triangular in section—*17th* **century**

259 A LEFT-HAND DAGGER, the hilt of russet steel damascened with scrolls in gold and silver azziminia, faceted pommel, straight hexagonal quillons **and** single knuckle ring, the grip curiously overlaid **with** silver-gilt bands and plaited with silver **wire**; the blade—10¼ *in. long*—trebly grooved and pierced—*Italian, 16th century*

> *Exhibited at the New Gallery, Early Italian Art,* **1894**
> *From the Breadalbane Collection*

260 A WHEEL-LOCK PISTOL, octagonal barrel fluted and ribbed at the base—*signed Lazarino Comminazzo*; the stock of **walnut**, finely mounted with chiselled and pierced steelwork **of an** interlaced floral design; the pommel, knuckle-guard **and** ramrod socket of steel, chiselled with birds, hounds and flowers; the ramrod terminating in a small bust; the lock chased with dolphins, acanthus leaves **and** fruit; the wheel ornamented in low relief with a figure **of a** merman, spirally fluted hook for attachment—16¼ *in.* **long**—*Italian, circa* 1640

> *From the Shandon Collection*
> *Exhibited at the New Gallery, Early Italian Art,* 1894
> **Vide** *Illustration*

261 A HANGER, the hilt of bronze, the pommel forms a lion's head, griffins and scrolls on the grip; the blade—28 *in. long*—back-edged and grooved—*17th century*

262 A CIRCULAR POWDER FLASK, of box-wood, gilt, carved **with a** spirited design **of a** huntsman, wild boar and two **hounds,** mounted with russet iron—*circa* 1615

> *From the Meyrick Collection*
> *Illustrated in Skelton*
> **Vide** *Illustration*

263 A CIRCULAR POWDER FLASK, of dark wood, engraved **with** annular designs **in** brass and stained ivory, curious **glass** centres, mounted with copper—*early 17th century*

> *From the Shandon Collection*

264 A SNAPHAUNCE PISTOL, the barrel partly octagonal, stock of dark wood with flattened butt, shaped pommel, and thistle ornaments in engraved brass, a snaphaunce lock, elaborately engraved with scrolls, brass lock plate, bearing the initials C. A., steel **and** brass ramrod, and hook for suspension— Scotch, circa **1620**

From the Londesborough Collection
Vide *Illustration*

265 A RAPIER, the hilt **of** bright steel, oviform pommel, slightly drooping quillons terminating in flattened knots, and double shell; the whole of the hilt finely chased in high relief with an equestrian encounter **in** the costume of *circa* 1635, the blade 30 *in. long*

From the Meyrick Collection

266 A BASKET-HILTED SWORD, inverted pear-shaped pommel, double knuckle and thumb ring, the whole of the hilt chiselled in low relief, decorated on either side with portraits, probably those of Charles I., strapwork borders terminating in hounds' heads, silvered and parcel-gilt; the blade—34 *in. long*— bearing the running wolf mark—*circa* 1640

From the Meyrick Collection
Engraved in Skelton

267 A PAIR OF BRIGHT STEEL SPURS, the necks and shanks finely chiselled with alternate scroll ornament, five-pointed rowels, double strap fastenings, and elaborately pierced buckles— *circa* 1630

From the Meyrick Collection
Engraved in Skelton

268 A RAPIER, of bright steel, oviform pommel, knuckle guard and straight quillons, pas-d'âne, double shell, and strong ricasso; the centre and ends of the knuckle bow chased with a winged dragon, the quillons terminating in equestrian figures, the pommel and shells chiselled and chased in high relief with a cavalry skirmish outside the walls of a town; the blade— 34 *in. long*—four-sided, grooved, and inlaid with the running fox mark in copper—*circa* 1640

From the *Meyrick Collection*

269 A HUNTING SWORD, entirely of bright steel, the pommel finely chiselled as a grotesque mask terminating in acanthus leaves, slightly swelling steel grip, fluted and enriched with eight raised ridges of roping, the knuckle **guard** and quillon in one piece terminating in female head, dolphin, and ornamented with a spirited design of acanthus leaves; the blade —34 *in.* long—six-sided, trebly grooved, and **pierced** with hearts **and** trefoils—*early 17th century*

    From the **Napier** *Collection*

270 A RAPIER, the **hilt of** bright steel of delicate workmanship, faceted globular **pommel**, slender curved quillons, knuckle guard, triple **bar and** fluted shells, **the** quillons, &c., **finely** notched; **the blade** — 48 *in.* long — stiff and four-sided, stamped with **the** armourer's mark, **a** crescent, on the ricasso —*circa* 1600

271 A RAPIER, the hilt of bright steel, curiously ridged and shaped pommel, surmounted by spirally roped tiddle, curved flattened quillons terminating in flattened cones, single bamboo-pattern ring, pas d'âne and counter guards, double shell, chiselled and pierced with foliage; the blade—42 *in.* long—six-sided, grooved **and** inlaid with the running fox mark in **copper, stamped with** the armourer's mark on the ricasso— *circa* 1610

    From the Meyrick Collection

272 A CARBINE HANGER, **of** bright steel, the **swivel** chiselled and chased with a double-headed serpent, **the rivet formed as a** spiral rosette, acanthus leaf knobs, the **loop above shaped as** double snakes **chased** in low relief, **with cone ornaments**— *Brescian, circa* 1640

    From the Shandon Collection

    Exhibited **at the** *New Gallery, Early* **Italian** *Art,* 1894

273 A CURIOUS **CLASP KNIFE**, the grip composed of plaques of brass engraved with monsters and scrolls; the blade of steel edged with brass, engraved with interlaced arabesque foliage — *Spanish, early part of the* 17th *century*

274 A GUN LOCK, of bright steel, elaborately chased and chiselled with grotesque figure, mask and griffin, also pierced with interlaced virated scroll—*circa* 1660

275 A SNAPHAUNCE GUN LOCK, of bright steel, the hammer chased with a mask and male figure, the iron supported by a lion, the groundwork engraved with hound, scrolls, &c.—*circa* 1670

276 A MORION, of blackened steel, with corded comb and drooping rim, a raised medallion on either side engraved with the Luscian arms—*early* 16th *century*

277 PORTIONS OF A PAGE'S SUIT, consisting of a tasset of six plates and part of an espalier, the rare form of decoration comprised of alternate bands of slashed and roped steel on an engraved groundwork richly gilt, studded with brass-headed rivets—*Italian, circa* 1525

> *From the Londesborough Collection*
> *Exhibited at the New Gallery, Early Italian Art,* 1894

278 A MORION, with graceful skull terminating in a four-sided spike, roped and slightly drooping brim, richly engraved with bands of trophies of arms and circular panels of male heads, gilt, the plume holder chased with a grotesque mask, the rivets round the base of the skull are curiously formed as four-sided spikes—*Italian, circa* 1560

> *From Lord Breadalbane's Collection*
> *Exhibited at the New Gallery, Early Italian Art,* 1894

279 A GORGET, of copper-gilt, finely embossed, chased with an equestrian encounter; on the right, warriors in Romanesque armour pursue retreating horsemen in Oriental costume, in borders of grotesque masks, military and musical trophies above, studded with copper-gilt rivets—*Italian, circa* 1640-50

> *Exhibited at the New Gallery, Early Italian Art,* 1894
> *From the Bateman Collection*
> *Vide Illustration*

280 A PAIR OF COUDRES OR ELBOW PIECES, of the highest quality, the decoration consists in an embossed and chiselled acanthus leaf, from either side of which issues a spirally coiled tendril terminating in a seeding flower, the work executed in bright steel relieved by russet borders, damascened scrolls, key pattern in gold, brass aillettes; attached are steel-plated straps damascened with scale design in gold and silver, showing their intended use to be worn over mail sleeves, dispensing with the rere and vambraces. These fine pieces of armour are in all probability the work of the Milanese armourer Paolo de Negroli—circa 1530–40—maker of the embossed breast-plate formerly in the Magniac Collection

From the Fountaine Collection
Exhibited at the New Gallery, Early Italian Art, 1894
Vide Illustration

281 THREE "PIÈCES DE RENFORT," consisting of demi-mentounière grande garde and bridle gauntlet; the latter two pieces are faceted, and with escalloped borders; the decorations of these pieces consists in bands of engravings: the mentounière with the figure of Atlas upholding the world, and Hercules struggling with the Hydra, a spray of acanthus foliage in the centre; the engraving on the grand garde and the gauntlet of similar character—*Spanish, circa* 1550

From the Uplands Hall Collection
Exhibited at the South Kensington Museum
Vide Illustration

282 A FLINT-LOCK PISTOL, entirely of bright steel, barrel partly octagonal, inscribed Pietro Palino—12½ in. long—the stock of steel engraved in four oblong panels with interlaced floral ornaments in annular-pattern borders, the pommel, trigger guard, base of barrel and ramrod socket finely chiselled and chased with acanthus leaves, masks and virating scrolls, the lock similarly ornamented—*signed Fiorintin*—19½ in. long—*Italian, circa* 1650

From the Shandon Collection
Vide Illustration

283 THREE "PIECES DE RENFORT," consisting of mentonnière, placcate and breast-plate; the mentonnière is secured to the breast-plate by three fluted screws; the placcate secured on the right-hand side of the mentonnière by nine small brass-headed rivets; the pieces are of bright steel, decorated on the breast-plate and placcate with radiating bands engraved with oval panels of Romanesque warriors supported by griffins, festoons, &c., gilt scroll borders; the mentonnière engraved with groups of leaf ornament, interlaced scrolls on the borders, gilt—*Spanish, circa* 1560

From the Ilam Hall Collection
Vide Illustration

284 A BREAST-PLATE, of bright steel, finely moulded tapul, roped turnover, and roped laminated gussets; the placcate fitting beneath the breast-plate and fitted with tasses of three plates curiously terminating in small tassets attached by riveted buckles; beneath the small tassets are fixed, by spring rivets, lobster tassets of eight plates, roped and sunk borders; the whole of this fine harness engraved in vertical bands in the style of Peter Speier; an oval panel on either breast, engraved on the right with The Crucifixion, on the left with a figure of a knight, kneeling, armed cap à pie, in the costume of *circa* 1530; beneath the turnover is engraved a battle of nude warriors; the other bands of engraving consisting in interlaced arabesques and scrolls

From the Pritchatt Collection
From the Bernal Collection
Vide Illustration

End of Second Day's Sale.

Third Day's Sale.

On THURSDAY, MARCH 10, 1898,

AT ONE O'CLOCK PRECISELY

JAPANESE CARVED IVORY NETSUKÉS.

291 DARUMA STRETCHING HIMSELF—*signed*; Momotaro and an Oni; Shokei and an Oni, seated in a boat drinking saké—*signed*; The Moral Courage of Kau-Shin   4

292 SHOKEI AND ONI; a Chinese sage; Diakoku seated on a bale; a stag and doe; a pilgrim; a man with the apparition horse 6

293 A PISTOL, russet iron barrel, damascened with the crest of the Prince of Satsuma

294 GAMA; Daruma; a boy polishing a temple stand; a Dutchman carrying a boy   4

295 AN INSECT STANDING ON A TILE, with vine leaves in relief—*signed*; a peasant filling her pipe; frog and lotos pod   3

296 A DUTCHMAN, with bow and arrow; a street dancer; long arms and long legs   3

297 A GROUP OF VEGETABLES; a pack ox and young; Shokei and Oni hiding in a tree trunk   3

298 HOTEI AND HIS BAG—*signed*; Fukurokujiu holding a kakémono and tortoise of longevity; Diakoku seated by his bag, and attendant rat—*signed*; Hotei holding a double gourd   4

299 A Boy and Pack Ox; two Oni hiding under a hat—*signed*; Ono-no Takamura and the toad—*signed*; Hotei carrying his bag and child—*signed*   4

300 Jurojin, Diakoku and Hotei seated round a tray of treasures—*signed*; a boat containing Yebishu and Diakoku fishing—*signed*; Kinko-a-Rishi on the carp   **3**

301 A Ball, formed as a Corean lion; a kylin and ball—*signed*; a fisherman; a bell and lotos leaf   4

302 A Tengu Hatching; a boy with Hotei's bag; Kinko-a-Rishi on the carp—*signed*; Gô-shisho with the apparition dragon   **4**

303 A Musumé, the dress delicately inlaid with circular crests in lead, stained ivory and lacquer; the treasure ship, of **ivory, wood and** mother-o'-pearl—*signed*; Urashima and **the sea** princess under a fir tree   3

304 A Treasure Ship, containing Bishamon, Diakoku, Benton, Hotei, Fukurokujiu, Yebishu and Jurojin; a monkey and octopus; Diakoku and giant radish   3

305 An Oni and Waves; Fukurokujiu and three children; a Dutchman, with bow and arrow; an Oni and temple gong   4

306 Diakoku and Hotei Wrestling; a Corean lion and young; **Takamura**; two Oni on ceremony—*signed*   4

307 A Bell—*signed*; children playing—*signed*; shells and octopus—*signed*; Jurojin and boy   4

308 Two Samourai—*signed*; Diakoku and rabbit; an itinerant show-man; Gama and toad   4

309 Momotaro—*signed*; Chinese children assisting the blind beggars—*signed*; Benton   **3**

310 Hotei discovered in his Bag by Children—*signed*; a work-man and puppy—*signed*; a fisherman and devil-fish; a temple bell—*signed*   4

311 A Prunus Grove and Storks; Shokei and attendant; an ojimé, carved with various autumn flowers; a skeleton   4

312 Kni-Taro, the infant giant; boy and drum; vines and pome-granates; Diakoku and Nô dancer   4

313 KIYO-HIMÉ WITH THE MONK AN-CHIN ; a pilgrim ; **Hotei—** *signed* ; Gama   4

314 FISHERMAN AND DEVIL-FISH ; Jobacko, carved with a priest ; a Damio jumping a go-bang board—*signed* ; Hotei and children—*signed*   4

315 A TEA-HOUSE, rocks, fir trees, Geisha and Musumé—*signed* ; fortified castle with moat—*signed*   2

316 A SHOWMAN ASLEEP, with a monkey ; **Takamura ; a court lady** with puppy ; a sage   4

317 SHOKEI ; Hotei and children ; Nō masks ; an Oni and rats   4

318 THE THOUSAND SPARROWS ; Chinaman ; street dancer **with** children ; group representing inrōs and netsukés   4

319 THREE SHŌJŌ ; Hotei with bag and boy ; physician ; Takamura   4

320 DARUMA ; an Oni playing a temple drum ; Nō dancer—*signed* ; a boy with pail of water   4

321 RATS IN A VENUS EAR SHELL ; a vegetable seller ; Hotei seated on his bag ; Shokei   4

NETSUKÉS (WOOD).

322 QUAILS AND MILLET SEED—*signed* ; rabbits ; a washerwoman ; a carp   4

323 TWO HORSES ; a boy and puppy forming a seal ; a gardener ; a Musumé, partly painted   4

324 AN ONI UPHOLDING A KORŌ ; a bamboo shoot and snail ; an ox 3

325 A THATCHED COTTAGE—*signed* ; an insect on a leaf ; a conch shell, from which issues the figure of a Samouri

326 A TEMPLE NIŌ **AND** BOY, partly coloured ; a skeleton—*signed* ; long arms and **long** legs ; mussels—*signed*   4

METAL WORK.

327 A Doctor's Baton, shaped as a dirk, of bronze, chased in **low** relief with emblematical ornaments and inlaid with flowering ornaments and dragons in gold—*signed*

328 Four Knife-Handles, of **shibuichi, inlaid with storks, quails,** vine foliage, prunus and **peonies in gold, silver, shakudo and** yellow **bronze**

329 A Pair of Small Upright Plaques, of shibuichi, inlaid **with cranes,** quails, and **flowers** in gold, silver and shakudo

330 A **Tsuba,** of russet iron, chased and inlaid in high relief with **three** ghosts in silver, copper and gold

331 A Tsuba, of russet iron, inlaid with a monkey in dress **of** ceremony of copper and silver, movable jaw—*signed*

332 An Oval Russet Iron Box, the cover decorated with four oval panels of translucent cloisonné enamel, flying fish, **fans and Hô-Hô** birds in the style Hirata Dōnin

333 A Silver Tea-Pot and Cover, pierced diaper ornaments on **the** handle and decorated with two raised silver-gilt loops, single, maple and other leaves, engraved **with a poem** in praise of tea, by Kiku Hozen of the Fô **dynasty in China—** *signed, Totsuô Dojin, aged eighty-three, of* **Great Japan**

334 A Silver Okimono, shaped as a korô, on **either side are two** shaped panels pierced and enamelled with **peonies, bamboo** and tiger lilies on a filigree ground, **dragon handles, the** cover chased with chrysanthemums—4½ *in.* **high—on a carved** ivory stand

335 A Long-Neck Bottle, at the base are four petal-shaped panels of shibuichi chased with peonies, chrysanthemums and wisteria, inlaid with gold and silver on a shakudo scroll-pattern filigree ground; around the centre and neck of the bottle are two bands of russet iron damascened with the key pattern in gold; silver-gilt liner—8½ *in. high*—on carved ivory stand

336 A GLOBULAR TRIPOD KORÔ AND COVER, **with** double handles,
of russet iron, on either side are two panels, the one decorated
with Minamoto-no-Yorimasa and the tiger, the other a coiled
dragon inlaid in two coloured golds on a wave-pattern
ground ; the whole **of** the groundwork minutely damascened
with annular ornaments and diaper patterns, the feet formed
as grotesque masks, the cover surmounted by a coiled
dragon in silver, **a** Chinese seal **character** below—5¾ **in.**
high

337 KORÔ incense-burner, wrought iron, with arabesques chased in
low relief, decorated with gold appliqué (kin-kise), cloisonné
and inlaid work ; the paulownia badge (go-san no **kiri**) in
gold inlaid, medallions representing chrysanthemums and
other flowers, &c., in cloisonné—*signed* Hirata Haruyuki,
with *Kakehan*

> *Exhibited at the **Fine Arts** Club, Japanese Exhibition*, 1894,
> **No. 21,** *Case* 6, *and illustrated in ' Notes on Shippo,' by*
> **J. L.** *Bowes, plate C, page* 93

OKIMONO IN WOOD AND IVORY.

338 AN OKIMONO, formed as Diakoku's hammer, containing a tee-to-
tum surmounted by the figure of a rat

239 A BOX AND COVER, formed as a figure of Jurojin seated on **a**
stork

340 A PAIR OF SPILL VASES, of ivory, basket pattern, entirely
carved in low relief with single and double chrysanthemums,
silver liners—*signed*—4 *in. high*

341 AN IVORY PIPE CASE, carved in high relief with dragons and
priests—*signed*

342 A PIPE CASE, of ivory, carved in low relief with a traveller
standing by a fir tree, after Hokusai—*signed*

343 A PIPE CASE, of polished stag's-horn, pierced and carved in low
relief with quails and millet **seed**

344 A SMALL OBLONG IVORY BOX, delicately lacquered with insects, and containing two smaller boxes shaped as fans

345 A PAIR OF LARGE IVORY TUSKS, carved in low relief with **the** Legend of Taka-Tsuna at the Battle of Ujigawa, partly inlaid with mother-o'-pearl, the plinths of wood carved **as** rocks—16¾ in. high by 6 in. diam.

346 AN OKIMONO, of the Ten Blind Beggars—*signed*

347 A SEAL, the top carved with frogs, lizards, tortoises and lotos leaves, inlaid with insects in mother-o'-pearl and stained ivory—*signed Seishu*

348 **AN** OKIMONO : the Legend of Shiba-on-ko and the Saké **Jar**—*signed*

349 A COOPER—*signed* ; Susano standing on the tortoise of long life, in **a** saké cup   2

350 A SKULL, around the top of which is coiled a lizard

351 AN OKIMONO : an artisan is seated beside a small table, chiselling a kodzuka, beside him stands a Musumé serving tea, implements and utensils around on the ground ; at the back a four-fold screen, on which is hung a basket of peonies, a gourd, the artisan's obei and fan

352 AN OKIMONO : an eagle holding in its talons a monkey—*signed*

353 AN OKIMONO : the mask carver—*signed* ; a group formed as six temple attendants moving a giant bell—*signed*   2

354 AN OKIMONO : an Oni carrying the shrine of Kwan-Non—*signed* ; an Oni carrying a bell and lantern—*signed*   2

355 AN OKIMONO : an Oni dressed as a retainer, presenting a shrine of Kwan-Non to a priest—*signed*

356 An Inrō, of ivory, in three divisions, decorated on one **side with a** helmet suspended from a prunus tree, with branches of peonies and wisteria, on the other side a vase of flowers formed as a Hō-Hō bird, the whole profusely inlaid in mother-o'-pearl, stained ivory, coral and tortoiseshell; the corners of silver with ornaments in translucent enamel, copper ojimé and ivory button netsuké, inlaid with Hotei yawning

357 A Gardener **and** Viper; and an **Oni and two young Oni,** hiding behind **a** hat

358 An Oni, pounding rice— *signed*

359 A Large Okimono, representing **the signs of the Zodiac—** *signed*

PORCELAIN.

360 A Satsuma Tea-Pot **and** Cover, with an upright panel of boys, fruit and flowers, enamelled in colours and gold—8 *in. high*

361 A Satsuma Bowl **and** Cover, painted with annular floral crest in colours and gold—6½ *in. diam.*

362 A Kutani Bowl, enamelled in yellow, purple and green **with** kiku flowers and Hō-Hō birds—7 *in. diam.*

363 A Pair of Square-Shaped Dishes, of similar china, enamelled with a cock, peonies and weeping willow—5½ *in. square*

364 An Imari Dish, the centre enamelled with a vase of peonies and **prunus, the outer** border composed of toku-shaped panels on **a blue ground,** the inner panel with four oval panels of **utensils on a** diapered-pattern ground—15 *in. diam.*

BRONZES.

365 **A** MIRROR-SHAPED JARDINIÈRE, on small feet, key-pattern borders
—signed, probably Seimin—4¾ in. diam.

366 **A** KORO AND COVER, formed as a pumpkin, surmounted by **the**
figure of a Mantis; and a koro and cover, on four monster
feet, surmounted by the figure of a kylin, diaper patterns **on**
the body—5¼ in. high   2

367 **A** KORO AND COVER, formed as a tortoise upholding **Urashima's**
box of longevity; and a small koro and cover, **formed as a**
lotos flower, surmounted by a leaf and kingfisher   2

368 THREE BRONZE KETTLES, one with spirit lamp

369 **A** VASE, formed as two folded lotus leaves, fine patina—4 in. **high,**
6 in. diam.
> Exhibited at the Fine Arts Club, Japanese Exhibition, 1894

370 **A** CYLINDRICAL VESSEL, the storm dragon in low relief, key
pattern on the borders, with the inscription, " Presented to
the Temple by one who was born in the year of the Rat, with
thanksgiving for the fulfilment of his request by the
Almighty "—7 in. high
> Exhibited at the Fine Arts Club, Japanese Exhibition, 1894

371 **A** SEATED FIGURE OF A MAN—6½ in. high

372 **A** SEATED FIGURE OF A PRIEST—4¼ in. high—signed

373 **A** WATER VESSEL, formed as a passion fruit ; and a small bronze
vase, formed as a folded tied lotos leaf

374 **A** VASE, formed as a wicker fishing-basket, a small crab on
exterior—6½ in. high

375 AN OVAL HANGING JARDINIÈRE, engraved with crabs, chains for
suspension ; and two bronze candlesticks, formed as lotos
and cranes   3

376 **A** CIRCULAR JARDINIÈRE, cloud design, chased in relief with
crescent moon and flying goose, key-pattern border—signed
Seimin—6⅛ in. **diam.**

377 A VASE, round the neck is coiled in relief a bifurcated dragon
—7 in. high

378 A VASE, formed as a tied brocade bag, the handles chased as
branches of prunus—7½ in. high

379 A PAIR OF ALTAR VASES, cylindrical bodies, fir-branch handles
and spreading open lips, chiselled in high relief with a sea-
shore scene with fishermen and Musumé, storm dragon at the
base, on diaper-pattern stand supported by Tongū—30 in.
high

380 A PAIR OF BRONZE ALTAR CANDLESTICKS, cylindrical vase-
shaped centres, decorated with upright panels with subjects
from the rice fields, the nozzle shaped as a peony, storm
dragon base chased with bands of key pattern and diaper
ornaments, three feet of cloud design—18½ in. high

381 A KORŌ, with three monster feet and large handles, pierced with
key pattern and leaf-shaped panels of emblematical ornaments
in low relief, the liner and cover surmounted by a figure of
a kylin—14 in. high

382 A LAMINATED CRAB, of russet iron—signed Miochin   2. 17. 6

CLOISONNÉ ENAMEL.

383 A PAIR OF FLAT-SHAPED OVIFORM CLOISONNÉ VASES, with
mirror-shaped panels of Hō-Hō, Shi Shi, dragon and kylin in
subdued colours on a dark buff ground—12¼ in. high

LACQUERS.

384 A SQUARE-SHAPED PICNIC BOX, in two divisions, in black lac,
with wisteria, peonies and chrysanthemums in raised gold—
9 in. by 8 in.—7 in. high

385 ANOTHER, nearly similar

386 A BOWL AND COVER, of gold nashiji, painted with sprays of chrysanthemums in raised gold, and plated with silver, the Tokugawa crest many times repeated—9 *in. diam.*

387 A CIRCULAR FLAT-SHAPED BOX, of Gouri lac, carved **with** conventional ornaments

388 A CIRCULAR RED LAC SAKÉ CUP, **with** a mountainous **lake** scene in gold ; and a smaller cup, of red lac, with Musumé cutting **a** maple branch

389 **A** GLOBULAR JAR AND COVER, of tortoiseshell lac, gold nashiji border, on earthenware—3¾ *in. high*

390 AN **OKIMONO, of** gold lacquer, shaped as an oviform saké **jar,** brocade cover, the groundwork decorated in flat golds **with** the kiri crests, cover and band of the kiku in raised **gold,** two jewel-shaped panels inlaid with lotos, chrysanthemums, peonies, hydrangea, wisteria and iris in mother-o'-pearl, tortoiseshell, stained ivory, coral and gold ; the handles of silver, chased as Oni heads holding rings ; feet formed of three attendants of the rats' wedding, in silver, their kimonos decorated with peonies in translucent enamels, **on** shaped wood stand lacquered **with** asters in **gold—6** *in. high*

391 A HABASHI, of coarse black and gold nashiji, **decorated in relief with** rolls of bamboo matting, rocks and **sprays of chrysan-**themums, plated with gold and silver, the **metal work of silver** pierced and embossed with peonies and **butterflies, the pipe** decorated with silver and gold damascened diaper ornaments

392 **A** SUZURI-BAKO WRITING BOX, nashiji, with decorations in gold lacquer **of** various shades in low relief, and Gyóbu mosaic ; chrysanthemums, rocks and clouds, **prunus** and flowing stream in interior—9½ *in.* by 10 *in.*—**18***th* **century**

Exhibited at the Fine Arts Club, **Japanese Exhibition, 1894,** No. 45, Case 15

393 A WRITING TABLE, en suite, mounted with **engraved silver—** 25 *in.* by **14** *in.,* 4¾ *in. high*

394 An Inrō, of natural wood, decoration consisting of lacquer of various colours in relief, faces inlaid in ivory, Yoshitsune and Benkei **on** the Gōjo bridge, Kiōto, wood button netsuké with gardening implements, and wood ojimé

*Exhibited at the **Fine** Arts Club, Japanese Exhibition,* 1894, *No.* 33, *Case* 20

395 A **YISSHU-KO-BAKO, box** for the **implements and articles** used in the game **of** perfumes (Kō-awasé); Taka-makiye on nashiji, with plum flowers in silver, and rocks, clouds, &c. **in** gyōbu; landscapes with the combination pine, **bamboo and plum;** inside of lid, chrysanthemums, lispedeza and **bamboo grass** (Arundinacea sp.), with dewdrops in silver

The game of perfumes (Kō-awasé) is an ancient game, which was confined to the court nobles and aristocracy, in which various kinds of incense were burnt in a ceremonial manner. The players had to guess the names of the incense or mixtures of incense burnt, and to indicate their decisions by means of the counters with which each was supplied. The incense was used in the form of a coarse powder previously made, or sometimes it was prepared during the game from fragrant woods, which were cut up with the implements (K) on the block (L). It was placed on a mica plate with a silver spoon. The plate was then held over the burning charcoal in the korō (E) with the silver forceps seen **in** (I) until it was thoroughly ignited and the perfume given off. **The** plate was then placed on one of the mother-o'-pearl knobs on the tray (H) to cool. When cold, the ash and unburnt portions were emptied into the box (N). Scented flowers were prohibited in the decoration of the room. No very trustworthy information can be obtained regarding all the details of the game, and the exact manner in which the counters and ruled board were used. There were evidently several modes of playing, but no complete account of them has been published in **any** known Japanese book.

The following articles and implements (A) *to* (N), *which belong to this box, are used in the game :—*

(A) Kiroku-suzeri, writing box used for making notes.

(B) Box for holding the "Ori-suye" (D).

(C) Kō-fuda-bako, box containing the counters (kō-fuda) in ten small receptacles.

The counters. There are 120 of these, divided into four series of thirty each. The counters of each series bear, respectively, the numerals 1, 2, 3, and the word "guest" (kyaku) on one face, and on the other face one of the following ten designs: The Japanese nightingale (cettia cantans), a willow, the asaram (asi), mandarin ducks, a cicada, crane, tortoise, chrysanthemum, the moon, and snow crystals. Thus in each

E

series of thirty there are three counters of each of these designs, viz.
three bearing a nightingale, three a willow, and so on. The counters
are of Shitan wood (Pterocarpus sp.) with the numbers and decorations
in gold and silver lacquer.

(D) Ori-suye, small folded bags of gilt paper or silk, in which the
incense is placed for use.

(E) Korō, small brazier, with cover in pierced silver, for **holding**
the burning charcoal over which the incense is heated.

(F) Fuda-zutsu, ivory vessel, in **the** shape of a bamboo stem, **in**
which **the** counters are placed by the players.

(G) Jū-kōgō, small box, in three tiers, for holding pieces of fragrant
woods and charcoal.

(H) Gin-dai, tray with thirteen mother-o'-pearl medallions **in** the
form of chrysanthemum flowers on nashiji. The mica plates
bearing the incense, after being heated over the brazier, are
placed on these to cool.

(I) Kō-saji-hi-suji-taté, silver stand, chased and pierced, for holding
the following implements: Gin-basami, silver forceps, by
which the mica plates (M) are held over the brazier (E).
Hay-osaye, a silver spatula used for arranging the ash upon
which the burning charcoal rests in the brazier. Hi-agi, a
small instrument said to be used for testing the heat of the
fire.

(J) Kō-ban, **a** board **ruled** in ten columns, each containing **ten**
rectangular spaces. The head of each column bears **the**
name of one of the ten designs found on the counters.

(K) Frame, in nashiji and kin-ji, for holding the following implements (Kō dōgu): Hi-bashi, "chop-sticks," used in arranging the charcoal in the brazier.

Ko-nokogiri, a saw.
Nomi, a chisel. ⎫ Used in cutting up and preparing
A small feather brush. ⎬ fragrant woods for use as in-
Ko-gatana, a knife. ⎭ cense.
Tetsu-kiné, a hammer.

(L) Kizami-ban, block, in Shitan wood, bound with silver, used **in**
cutting up woods for incense.

(M) Gin-ban, mica plates, ten in number, with silver edges, upon
which the incense is burnt.

(N) Taki-gara-iré, vessel, in the form of a bamboo stem, for receiving
the ashes of the burnt incense.

The lacquer articles are in kin-ji, makiye and nashiji, with landscapes and decorations corresponding with those on the large box I.

Exhibited at the Fine Arts Club, Japanese Exhibition, 1894,
No. 1, *Case* 14

396 A SQUARE-SHAPED BOX, of gold nashiji, with sprays of peonies
and kiku badge in raised gold—5½ *in.* by 6 *in.*—18*th century*

397 A Box, shaped as two shells, of flat gold lac, the concave shell
decorated with a house and river scene

398 An Octagonal Inrō, of black lac, engraved and powdered in gold
with horses—*signed*

399 An Inrō, of gold lac, with a seated figure of Jurojin and his stag
—*signed*

400 A Gold Lac Inrō, decorated with a mountain waterfall in
raised gold and mosaic, a sage and **boy,** inlaid in gold, silver,
shakudo and shibuichi—*signed*

401 A Kōdai Stand, for the implements and articles for the "game
of perfumes," rich gold nashiji ground, arabesque foliage in
raised gold, above this again are sprays of peonies in plates of
gold and kin-makayi, circular badge of the Tokugawa family
many times repeated—11 *in.* by 9 *in.*, 12 *in. high—early
18th century*

> *Exhibited at the Fine Arts Club, Japanese Exhibition, 1894,
> No. 22, Case 14*

402 A Hexafoil-Shaped Habashi, with pierced **silver cover, en**
suite

403 A Ryō-shi-Bunko Manuscript Box, nashiji, with decorations of
gold lacquer in two shades, and silver lacquer, gyōbu inlay of
gold and silver in mosaics of squares and small **rods;** on
the lid, in the foreground, a small Shintō shrine, **divided by**
a swift river from a village of rude cottages; above this rises
a mountain side covered with cherry trees in **blossom** and
other fruit trees, from behind which appear the roofs of the
buildings of a Bhuddhist temple, similar landscapes round
the sides; inside plain nashiji—19½ *in.* by 12¼ *in.—18th
century*

> *Exhibited at the Fine Arts Club, Japanese Exhibition, 1894,
> No. 7, Case 15*

404 A SUZUMI BAKO WRITING BOX, the margins of pewter (okiguchi), inside of lid nashiji, passing gradually into plain gold and again into gyōbu mosaic ; decoration, gold lacquer in relief, rocks of gyōbu mosaic with pines and flowering cherry trees overhanging a waterfall ; outside of lid similar material **with** silver gyōbu mosaic ; and within the box a Mizu-ire in the form of a " treasure ship " (Takara-bune) ; holder of ink cake (Sumi-hasami) ; knife and puncturing-needle (Kiri), of nashiji lacquer with silver mounts—10¾ in. by 10 in.—18th century

Exhibited at the Fine Arts Club, Japanese Exhibition, **1894,** *No.* 30, *Case* 15

405 AN INRŌ, polished black lacquer ground ; decoration, lacquer in relief and incrustation of mother-o'-pearl and shibuichi. Tōba (Chinese poet of the 11th century) riding on mule back—*signed* KAJIKAWA, and, for the metal work, YŌI (died 1760)

Exhibited at the Fine Arts Club, Japanese Exhibition, 1894, *No.* 4, *Case* 12

406 A CIRCULAR BOX, on three legs, in the **shape** of a Hokai (for holding rice), gold nashiji, chrysanthemums and other floral decorations in raised gold, mounted in gilt copper

Exhibited at the Fine Arts Club, Japanese Exhibition, **1894,** *No.* 9, *Case* 13

407 A CHI-KE, of shaded gold lac, shaped as a persimmon fruit

408 AN INRŌ, formed as a war fan, of flat gold lac, decorated with a prunus tree in blossom ; Oni and Tengu sporting and performing acrobatic feats, inlaid in mother-o-pearl, stained ivory tortoiseshell and coral—*signed*—the wooden netsuké shaped as an Oni polishing a joey, russet iron ojimé, inlaid with a tiger lily in gold and silver

409 An Octagonal Inrō, of flat gold lac, inlaid with Shōkei and Oni
performing acrobatical feats, background of prunus and
gladiola in mother-o'-pearl, stained ivory, coral and tortoiseshell—*signed*—ivory netsuké carved as clouds, with a coiled
dragon in silver and gold, russet iron ojimé, shaped as a lotos
pod and inlaid in gold and silver

410 An Oblong Tray, Taka-Makiye, inlay of gyōbu, silver, mother-
o'-pearl and coral; border, diapers with kiku flowers,
landscape of the Chinese school, bound in pewter—13 *in.* by
6¼ *in.*—17th century

Exhibited at the Fine Arts Club, Japanese Exhibition, 1894,
No. 26, *Case* 10

411 A Double Square-Shaped Box, the upper one of black lacquer
with branches of peonies in raised gold, the lower box of
dead gold, decorated with conventional water pattern, nashiji
interior—5 *in.* by 3½ *in.*

412 A Chi-re, formed as an egg plant, gold lacquer, fine nashiji
interior

CHINESE OBJECTS OF ART.

413 A Carved Agate Cup and Saucer

414 A Pair of Old Cloisonné Enamel Cylindrical Vases, with
chrysanthemums, convolvulus and prunus in colours on a
turquoise-blue ground, Hō-Hō birds and utensils on the neck
on a marble-pattern ground, key pattern on the neck and
base—18 *in.* high

415 A Pair of Cloisonné Enamel Cylindrical Vases, with
branches of chrysanthemums, peonies and rocks in colours
on a white key-pattern ground, turnips and insects on the
neck on a red ground—15½ *in.* high

416 A Canton Enamel Bowl, Cover and Stand, painted with
conventional flowering aster in colours on an imperial yellow
ground—6 *in.* diam.

417 A SMALL BOTTLE, of marbled yellow and brown glass

418 A CARVING, of pale green jade, the figure of a fisherman **holding** in his right hand a net, in his left a fish—5¾ *in. high*

419 A SMALL CARVING, of pale green jade, formed as the figure of a boy seated on a double gourd

420 A CIRCULAR PENDANT, of pale green jade, cloud ornament above, a revolving figure of a boy in the centre

421 AN OCTAGONAL BOX AND COVER, of pale **green jade, the edges** incised with double lines—*Indian*

422 A **PAIR** OF GLOBULAR VASES, of **cloisonné enamel, peonies and rocks** in colours **on a black key-pattern ground,** conventional asters and leaf ornaments on the neck—10¾ *in.* **high**

CHINESE ENAMELLED PORCELAIN.

423 A FAMILLE VERTE DISH, the centre divided into four fan-shaped panels with stags, cocks, badgers and ducks, conventional asters in red on the border—11 *in. diam.*

424 A PAIR OF PLATES, enamelled with a five-clawed dragon, **sacred** jewel and flames in coral colour and **gold** on **a green wave-**pattern ground—7½ *in. diam.*

425 A PAIR OF FAMILLE VERTE DISHES, mirror-shaped panels in the centres, rocks and cherry blossoms on the borders

426 A FAMILLE VERTE DISH, enamelled in the centre with a circular panel of a **kylin** and Hô-Hô bird, fruit-shaped panels on the border, of utensils on a flowered mauve ground

427 AN OCTAGONAL FAMILLE ROSE DISH, enamelled in the **centre** with **a** cock, rocks and peonies, shaped panels of **utensils on** a pink and green diapered ground

428 A FAMILLE VERTE DISH, enamelled with a basket of flowers in the centre, panels of lotos and other flowers on the border ; and a plate, with birds and weeping willow in the centre

429 A FAMILLE VERTE DISH, enamelled in the centre with a circular panel, floral ornaments on a buff ground, sprays of lotos and peonies **on** the border

430 A NANKIN DISH, with radiating petal-shaped panels of flowers on a diaper-pattern ground

431 A DISH, decorated with floral ornaments **in the** Imari taste

432 A PAIR OF FAMILLE VERTE DISHES, in **the** centre are ladies and children dancing on a terrace, **palm** trees, balconies and utensils in the foreground, eight sacred jewel shaped panels of utensils on the border, on various diapered and trellised grounds—14½ *in. diam.*

433 A PAIR OF OCTAGONAL FAMILLE ROSE DISHES, with leaf-shaped **panel in the centres,** enamelled with peonies and rocks over **which is drawn a half** unrolled kakémono, disclosing a branch **of prunus and birds, the** borders covered with ammonite scrolls **in sepia, and further** enriched with bamboo, peonies **and prunus** in enamel—13 *in. diam.*

434 A PAIR OF RICE-JARS AND COVERS, **painted with alternate sprays** of prunus, lotos, fir **and peonies in famille verte,** copper-gilt handles—6¾ *in. high*

435 A PAIR OF CYLINDRICAL VASES AND COVERS, the whole of the body entirely covered **with** conventional floral ornaments in brilliant colours, **leaf pattern** on the necks and bases, four coral-coloured loops for suspension, pale blue and pink **borders,** blue interiors—*Kien Lung Dynasty*—13 *in. high*

436 A FAMILLE ROSE DISH, the decoration in the centre **consists** of a procession of ladies with flowing draperies, **a horse, on** which is seated another lady on a pillion, passing through **a** trellis arch overgrown with foliage, cherry trees, bamboo and peonies in **the** distance; the border **is ornamented with four** quatrefoil-shaped panels of peonies, chrysanthemums **and lotos on a** diaper-pattern ground—21¾ *in. diam.*

437 A PAIR OF FAMILLE ROSE **DISHES, of the** highest quality, the centres enamelled with **branches** of pink and yellow peonies, double chrysanthemums, prunus, butterflies **and** grasshoppers, the borders similarly decorated with peonies in four groups, narrow outer border with conventional lotos flowers on a pink ground, narrow inner border of petal ornaments and bands of yellow—21 *in. diam.*

SELF COLOUR.

438 A PAIR OF BOWLS AND COVERS, of apple-green crackle, on open dark wood stands—4 *in. diam.*

439 A PAIR OF BOTTLES, of apple-green crackle—5 *in. high*—on dark wood stand

440 A BOTTLE, of turquoise crackle—12 *in. high*

441 ANOTHER, of similar colour, engraved with a conventional peony under the glaze—11 *in. high*

End of Third Day's Sale.

Fourth Day's Sale.

On FRIDAY, MARCH 11, 1898,

AT ONE O'CLOCK PRECISELY.

OBJECTS OF ART OF XVIITH AND XVIIITH CENTURIES.

450 A BULL-DOG'S HEAD, carved in ebony, forming a box, mounted with silver

451 A SHELL-SHAPED GOLD VINAIGRETTE, enamelled with dark blue and white stripes

452 A PEAR-WOOD SPOON, with shell-shaped bowl carved with acanthus foliage, and fluted handle terminating in a grotesque mask, cornucopiæ and shield-shaped ornaments—18th century

453 A SILVER-GILT NEEDLE CASE, finely chased in relief with terminal female figures, medallions, festoons of laurel, &c., brilliant clasp—French, temp Louis XIV.

454 A SILVER ETUI CASE, embossed and chased with figures, flowers and scrolls, fitted with compasses, &c.—French, temp Louis XV.

455 CUPID CROWNING A FRENCH POODLE WITH A GARLAND OF FLOWERS : a circular wax relief—signed Cadet de Beaupré, 1789—4½ in. diam.—in glazed ebonised frame

456 A PAIR OF OBLONG MINIATURES, painted in grisaille with subjects from La Fontaine's Fables, in black frames

457 A SMALL FOLDING CORKSCREW, of bright steel, chased with scrolls on a matted gold ground—*temp* Louis XV.

458 A CURIOUS SILVER PEN-CUTTER, by Edward Amory, of London, slightly moulded borders—18*th century*

459 A GREEN SHAGREEN CASE, containing a pair of knives, one with steel and one with silver blade, the **handles** of ivory **with** grooved gold ferrules and shell-shaped pommels—7½ *in.* **long** —*temp* Louis XVI.

460 A GREEN SHAGREEN CASE, containing a steel-bladed knife, the handle composed of plaques of mother-o'-pearl finely mounted in ribbed gold ; fitting within the knife is a smaller folding knife, with gold and steel blade, inscribed *Conseil Caen*—9½ *in. long—length of smaller knife* 7 in.—*French, temp* Louis XVI.

461 A PAIR OF EGYPTIAN PORPHYRY TAZZE, mounted with chased or-molu, **in the** style of Gouthière, on tripod altar stands, very finely chased with goats' heads and feet, festoons of roses and other flowers, bands of laurel ornaments, rosettes and scale chasings—4½ *in. high* by 5 *in. diam.*

Vide Illustration

VIENNA PORCELAIN.

462 A CUP AND SAUCER, painted in bands of **laurel foliage in gold** on a maroon and buff ground
From the Bohn Collection

463 A CUP AND SAUCER, the cup painted with an upright panel **of Leda and** the Swan, on a groundwork of two shades **of** mauve, decorated with arabesque ornaments in gold
From the Bohn Collection

464 A CUP AND SAUCER, the cup painted in grisaille with an **oval** portrait of the Duchess of York, by Schaller, on a ground of alternate bands of green, gold and white, raised gilding
*From the **Bohn** Collection*

465 A CUP AND SAUCER, the cup painted with a circular medallion of Venus and Cupid in brilliant colours on a dark maroon ground, vine ornament and arabesques in raised gold

From the Bohn Collection

466 **A** CUP AND SAUCER, the cup painted with an oval medallion after Angelica Kauffman, groundwork of bands of dark mauve and green key pattern and scrolls in raised gold

From the Bohn Collection

467 A CUP AND **SAUCER**, **painted** with **an oval medallion of a dancing nymph and** Bacchanalian **figures, and a groundwork of dark green, mauve and gold**

From the Bohn Collection

468 **A** CUP AND SAUCER, **with bands** of gros-bleu, key pattern in gold

From *the Bohn Collection*

469 A CUP AND SAUCER, the cup painted with an upright panel of Cupid overcoming a lion, on a pale green ground with doves and laurels in gold, panels of dark maroon with acanthus foliage in raised **gold**

From the Bohn **Collection**

DRESDEN PORCELAIN.

470 A PAIR OF DRESDEN PORCELAIN TAZZE, formed as draped **female** figures supporting openwork baskets, fluted plinths **with key** pattern in low relief, baskets and plinths painted with **festoons** of flowers—14½ **in.** *high*

471 AN OVAL DRESDEN PORCELAIN SNUFF-BOX, painted **on the** exterior **with** equestrian encounters, the interior of **the lid** painted with **a** portrait of Frederick **the** Great, in blue dress, crimson and ermine cloak, and wearing the Order of the Black Eagle, mounted with engraved gilt metal—3¼ *in.* by 2½ *in.*

472 A FINE ECUELLE, COVER AND STAND, the dish painted in the
centre in the style of old Hizen, three oblong panels of landscapes, buildings, cattle and figures, on a gold and mauve
trellis groundwork; the ecuelle painted on the cover with
three quatrefoil-shaped panels of landscapes, figures and
cattle, on a groundwork of scrolls, figures and strap ornaments in the Chinese taste; the handle forms the figure of a
squirrel; the base of the ecuelle curiously enamelled with
arabesque ornaments in yellow, blue and mauve—6 *in. diam.*

ENGLISH PORCELAIN.

473 A CHELSEA FIGURE OF NEPTUNE, standing on a dolphin, richly
painted robe, and holding in his right hand a trident, on
scroll plinth encrusted with shells and seaweed—9½ *in. high*

474 A PAIR OF PORCELAIN BUSTS, of a male and female Bacchante,
on octagonal pedestals with decorations in gold—4¼ *in. high*
—on ebony plinths

475 A CANDLESTICK, made by Minton, 1875, in imitation of " Faience
de St. Porchaire" (Henry II. ware), architectural in form,
grotesque masks, statuettes, festoons of laurels and cherubs,
heads, arabesque ornaments in brown, green, red and black—
signed, *C. Toft*—13¼ *in. high, the base* 7½ *in. diam.*

476 A BLACK BASALT CUP AND SAUCER, with figures in low relief,
striped base; and a cup and saucer, with Cupids sporting in
white on a pale blue ground

SÈVRES PORCELAIN.

477 A DIAMOND-SHAPED TRAY, painted in the centre with an oval panel containing a spray of roses, the border ornamented with small oval panels formed of festoons of laurels and turquoise beads, each compartment containing a small flower, outer borders of bleu-de-roi with œils-de-perdrix decoration in gold, by **Lecot (?)**

XVTH XVITH AND XVIITH CENTURY OBJECTS OF ART.

478 A PAIR OF SCISSORS, of russet steel, with hexafoil-shaped rings, and double groove on the back of the blades, the whole damascened and overlaid with arabesque foliage in gold—*Persian*—11¼ *in. long*

479 A SMALL UPRIGHT PLAQUE, of bright steel, chased in relief with the infant figure of St. John, cherubs' heads at the corners—*16th century*—3½ *in.* by 2¼ *in.*

480 A STEEL PLAQUE, slightly embossed with figures of Hercules and nymph in a garden, overlaid and damascened in gold—3¾ in. **by** 3¾ *in.*—*Italian, 16th century*

481 A FIRE STRIKER, **of** bright steel, formed as an oval shield, supported on either side by gardant lions, cornucopiæ, and surmounted by a winged dragon—*French, 17th century*

482 A FIRE STRIKER, of bright steel, chased in low relief with a **double-headed** eagle crowned—*16th century*; and one, shaped **as a shell, with** laurel foliage borders, and chased with **Medusa's head in** low relief in the centre—*16th century*

483 A Scissor Case, **of bright** steel, engraved with interlaced floral foliage, a **crown,** double heart and clasped hands; above is a ribbon engraved "NOUS SOMMES INSEPARABLES," on the other side a figure of Cupid and the inscription— JAN + PEUT + DISPOSER—*temp* Louis XIII.

484 Another, engraved **with a pelican in her piety, with motto** below, flowers and **scrolls on the groundwork—***17th century***;** and one, of similar **form, engraved with Cupid fishing for** hearts, with a motto **engraved above—**

"JAOUN NE MA'IAMAIS ECHAPÉ

JE ME REND MAISTRE DE TOUT."

17th century

485 A Signet Ring, of bright steel, chiselled and chased in high relief, the oval cartouche in the centre is supported on either side by mermaids with uplifted arms and intertwined tails, on either side are the masks of grotesque marine monsters, festoons of laurel and acanthus foliage—*Italian, 16th century*

486 A Small Scissor Case, **of russet iron, inlaid with pelicans,** snakes, rosette and **beaded** ornaments in silver—*English,* **late** *16th century*

487 A Small Circular Flat-Shaped Water Flask, of maplewood, mounted with silver pierced with Gothic ornaments and with strawberry leaf edging, the base forming a seal with reversed cypher L. L.—*16th century*

From *the Shandon Collection*

488 A Knife, the hilt of steel, chiselled as a partly draped figure of Venus, the blade 4 *in. long*, back-edged—*Italian, 16th century*

N.B. *The spoon and fork, with Vulcan and Cupid, are in the South Kensington Museum*

From the Shandon Collection

489 A GOBLET, manufactured by Messrs. Philips for the 1851
Exhibition : the cup engraved with panels formed of interlaced branches containing owls and other birds, the circular
base engraved with acanthus leaves, the stem and base of
the cup mounted in chased and pierced silver of Gothic
design, depressed fluted knob in the centre of amethyst—
6½ in. high

490 A STEEL SHUTTLE, finely pierced with scroll **foliage—*late* 17th**
century
From the Shandon Collection

491 A STEEL MOUNT OF AN ESCARCELLE, opening in three divisions,
the catches chased with lions' masks holding rings—
Nuremberg—middle of 16th century

492 A FLEMISH KNIFE CASE, of box-wood, carved in ten panels with
Scriptural subjects in relief, inscription and date 1589 **on** the
sides
From the Shandon Collection

493 ANOTHER, similar, with **a** monk's head in relief, pierced for suspension, roped edges, carved with initials w.G.w., and date
1593
*From the Bernal **and Shandon** Collections*

494 A KNIFE AND FORK **CASE,** with Scriptural subjects in ten compartments, and inscriptions—   .

      " WAT ' GHY ' DOET ' DENCKT ' OP ' HETENT "

and   " WAER ' DATGHY ' SYT ' V ' SELVENKE "

From the Shandon Collection

495 A KNIFE SHEATH, **carved** in eight compartments with **subjects**
from the life of Moses, and engraved with inscriptions

*It formerly belonged to the Dutch Governor of Pedang in
the island of Sumatra, from whom it fell into the hands of a
Malay chief, and was brought from India by Capt. W. Parker
in 1807*

From the Magniac Collection

496 A HEART-SHAPED RELIQUARY, of box-wood, minutely pierced and carved with The Annunciation and The Crucifixion, and mounted with silver-gilt filigree frame and small enamelled rosette loop—*Russian*, 17*th century*

497 A FOLDING SPOON, the bowl and handle of cowrie shell, mounted with silver chased with masks and scroll ornaments, forming a fork—17*th century*

From the Londesborough Collection

498 ANOTHER, of tortoiseshell, with chased **silver mount forming a** fork—17*th* **century**

499 AN OVAL SNUFF-BOX, of box-wood, delicately carved with interlaced acanthus foliage—*French*, 18*th century*

500 A BOX, of box-wood, carved as an infant Triton riding a dolphin —*late* 17*th century*

501 A WARRIOR'S HEAD, wearing a barbuta or salade, carved from a nut—16*th century*—on ebonised pedestal

502 AN ELIZABETHAN MOTTLED JUG, mounted with silver rim, foot and cover, the billet formed as a grotesque mask, the cover embossed in three strapwork panels with male and female busts and pendant bunches of fruit, the foot mount chased and embossed with egg and tongue ornament, strawberry leaf piercing at the edge, below the billet is a coat-of-arms engraved with the initials c. f. and v. b. and the date 1541— 8½ *in. high*

503 AN UPRIGHT BRONZE-GILT PLAQUE, decorated in relief with a figure **of** Mary bearing the dead Christ—7½ *in.* by 5½ *in.*— *Italian*, 16*th century*

Exhibited at the New Gallery, Early Italian Art, 1894

504 A "MONTRE SOLAIRE," of copper-gilt and blued steel, finely pierced and engraved with acanthus foliage, engraved with many numerals and names of towns

505 A KNIFE AND TWO-PRONG FORK, steel blade, brown Botcher handles—17*th* **century**

507 A SET OF FOUR KNIVES, the handles formed as Corinthian columns, surmounted by leaf-pattern knobs overlaid with plaques of mother-o'-pearl

508 **A** PEWTER TANKARD, curiously decorated with strap ornaments, Romanesque warriors, baskets and vases of fruit and flowers, inlaid in brass, scroll handle and brass billet—14¾ *in. high*— *English, early 17th century*

Exhibited at the South Kensington Museum

509 A TRIANGULAR INK-STAND, of metal-gilt, the sides finely engraved with a vase, festoons of fruit and flowers on either side suspended from lions' heads, nude male figures, griffins and Satyrs, on three small feet, the cover surmounted by a small figure of Cupid—*circa* 1600

From the Shandon Collection

510 A SMALL SHALLOW BOWL, of Limoges enamel, with open scroll handle, the centre painted in grisaille with Ariadne, in borders of scroll foliage and birds in translucent colours and gold, the back painted with a village scene in colours—*signed* J. L. (Jean Laudin)—5 *in. diam.*

From Lord Hastings' Collection

511 A FLAT BOWL, painted in grisaille and flesh tints with a sheep-shearing subject, with the sign of the scorpion above, heightened with gold, and with masks and arabesques on the back—6¼ *in. diam.*—by Jean Cortois

From Lord Hastings' Collection

512 AN OBLONG INK-STAND, of silver-gilt, containing two ink-vases and an oblong box, the top and portions of the side finely chased and pierced with interlaced scrolls; the whole mounted with oval and oblong panels of rock-crystal engraved and silvered with rosette flowers and acanthus leaves, silver-gilt roped edges, supported on four small lion feet—12 *in. long*, 6 *in. wide*, 4½ *in. high*

513 A SMALL CYLINDRICAL ROCK-CRYSTAL CUP AND COVER, mounted with silver-gilt, and with a terminal female figure on the handle—4 *in. high*

From the Magniac Collection

F

514 A KNIFE AND TWO-PRONGED FORK, the **handles** of silver-gilt **finely** pierced and chased with figures of boys, foliage, &c.— *in case—17th century*

515 A BELT, of silver, partly gilt, of **close** interlaced links, **rosette** fastenings and hinges, gilt, chased and pierced with masks, acanthus foliage, &c.—16 oz. 6 dwt.—*Augsburg, 17th century*

516 A SPOON, of maple-wood, mounted with copper-gilt chased with strapwork, masks, &c., surmounted by the figure of an apostle —*German, 16th century*

517 A KNIFE, DOUBLE-PRONGED FORK AND SILVER-GILT SPOON, the handles of silver filigree—*17th century*

518 A SMALL SILVER FIGURE OF A SPHINX, with draped head—*16th century*

519 A COCOANUT **CUP,** mounted with circular foot, rim and **bands of** ribbed and roped silver, the cocoanut carved in three panels, with oval medallion portraits of gentlemen—6½ *in.* high— *17th century*

520 A COCOANUT CUP AND COVER, mounted with metal-gilt—12 *in.* high—*German, 16th century*—double circular base embossed with masks and strapwork, supported on three griffin feet, vase-shaped stem, the straps chased in relief with figures, &c., egg and tongue ornament round the neck, and engraved with interlaced foliage, the cover similarly ornamented, surmounted by a small helmeted figure

521 Two GOLD MOUNTS, chased and chiselled as cherubs' heads, richly enamelled in translucent colours; and A GROUP OF FRUIT AND FLOWERS, of similar workmanship

These three pieces of goldsmith's work were formerly part of the decoration of a chalice, said to be by Cellini (see correspondence).

From the Poniatowski Collection

RHODIAN DISHES.

522 **A Dish**, painted with sprays of roses, bluebells, &c. in brilliant colours—12 *in. diam.*

523 A FLATTENED DISH, circular panel in the centre, conventional, arabesques around—14 *in. diam.*

524 A DEEP DISH, painted with pink carnations, bluebells, &c., heightened with gold—14 *in. diam.*

525 A RHODIAN DISH, with arabesque scale patterns in red and blue on a green scale-pattern ground, ammonite scrolls on the border—11¼ *in. diam.*

526 A RHODIAN DISH, curious **ornament and flowers in green compartments**—11½ *in. diam.*

    Said by Dr. Badger to represent the wings of Allah

527 **A Deep Dish**, with shaped edges, the centre painted with carnations and conventional flowers in brilliant red and blue, ammonite scroll and shell border—11½ *in. diam.*

528 A DISH, with spirited interlaced arabesques in red and blue on a green ground in the centre, leaf-pattern border—12 *in. diam.*

529 A DISH, with sprays of carnations and bluebells in the centre, ammonite scrolls on the border—11¾ *in. diam.*

530 **A** DISH, with four sprays of carnations, arabesque ornaments in red and blue, ammonite scroll borders—10¼ *in. diam.*

---

531 A DEEP MAJOLICA DISH, finely painted in brilliant colours with a rocky river scene, buildings and bridge, oval shield-of-arms at the top—9½ *in. diam.*—in dark wood frame

532 THE COMPANION

F 2

OLD ITALIAN AND FRENCH BRONZES.

533 VENUS DE MEDICI: a bronze statuette—15 *in. high*

534 ANTINOUS: the companion—15 *in. high*

535 A PAIR OF BRONZE STATUETTES, of a boy and infant Satyr, carrying an owl and dog—14¼ *in. high—French*

536 A PAIR OF CIRCULAR BRONZE PEDESTALS, decorated in relief with Bacchus, Satyrs, nymphs and animals, Brocatelle marble capitals and plinths—8 *in. high—late 17th century*

537 THE FIGHTING GLADIATOR—9 *in. high*—on bronze plinth

538 THE FIGHTING GLADIATOR—11 *in. high*—on black marble plinth

539 HERCULES HURLING LYCHAS INTO THE SEA: a spirited bronze —16¼ *in. high*

540 A PAIR OF SNUFFERS, of Honey bronze, decorated with grotesque winged mask terminal figures, fruit and flowers—*Italian, 16th century*

541 AN ANTIQUE STATUETTE OF AN ATHLETE, leaning on a club— 7½ *in. high*

542A BRONZE MEDALLION, of Italian work—*end of the 16th century.* *Obv.* head of Hercules to right, wearing oak wreath and the lion's skin knotted round neck; *rev.* Hercules in antique costume to right, receiving from Hylas, who is also clad as a warrior, the robe of Nessus; in the exergue H B (*mon*) and an eagle—attributed to Corvino after an engraving by Hans Sebald Beham—*very fine*—1½ *in. diam.*

  From the His de la Salle Sale

543 A BULL—*Italian, 16th century*—on veined red and green marble plinth—5 *in. high,* 6¾ *in. long*

544 A PAIR OF FIGURES OF PEASANTS, one bag-piping—*late 17th century*—on ebonised plinths mounted with metal-gilt—7 *in. high*

545 A STATUETTE OF AN ATHLETE, his toga draped over his right shoulder, fluted plinth—7½ *in. high*

546 A STATUETTE OF A WRESTLER—*Italian, early 16th century—* 6½ *in. high*—on giallo marble plinth

547 A MORTAR, with curiously plaited handles and raised spear ornaments—*signed Davcrazzo Bartolomeo, and dated* 1420— 6½ *in. diam.,* 14¼ *in. high*

549 A GROUP, of two infant Bacchanals and Satyr riding a goat, on Louis XV. plinth of chased or-molu of scrolls and flowers— 7¼ *in. high*

From Lord Clancarty's Collection

550 A CIRCULAR PLAQUE, of bronze-gilt, embossed and chased **in the** centre with The Judgment of Solomon, acanthus leaf **and** bead-pattern border—3½ *in. diam.*

551 A BRONZE KNOCKER, the clapper formed as an infant Triton, supported by dolphins and suspended by a grotesque mask of a marine deity—*Italian, 16th century*—12 *in. high*

552 A SMALL BRONZE BUST, of the Saviour, on wood stand—*Italian, 16th century*—3¾ *in. high*

From the His de la Salle Collection

553 A SEATED BRONZE FIGURE OF AGRIPPINA, with flowing drapery, fine green patina—3 *in. long by* 3½ *in. high*—16*th century*— on Egyptian porphyry plinth

Exhibited at the New Gallery, Early Italian Art, 1894
From the His de la Salle Collection

554 A PAIR OF BRONZE BUSTS OF NEGROES, with open mouths, forming door knobs—*Italian, 16th century*—4 *in. high*—on ebonised pedestals

From the Wells Collection

555 PERSEUS: a bronze of fine patina—*Italian, 16th century*—11¼ *in. high*

556 MERCURY, playing a flute, a cloak draped from the left shoulder over the right arm—*Italian, 16th century*—on metal and black marble plinth—8¾ *in. high*

From General Buller's Collection
Vide Illustration

557 A PAIR OF FIGURES OF DANCING BOYS, playing a triangle and tambourine—8½ *in. high*—*French, 18th-century*

558 FLORA, seated on a pedestal, holding flowers in her right hand, an Italian bronze of fine patina—*end of 16th century*—12¾ *in. high*—on black marble pedestal, circular red and green marble plinth
From General Butler's Collection
Vide Illustration

559 THE WRESTLERS: an important bronze group—16½ *in. high*—*French, 17th century*—on circular giallo marble plinth—12 *in. high*—on veined scagliogla column—33 *in. high*
From the Godding Collection
Vide Illustration

560 A PAIR OF GROUPS, of Bacchus, Satyrs and nymphs—7½ *in. high*—*French, 17th century*—on circular black marble plinths
From Lord Clancarty's Collection
Vide Illustration

561 THE FARNESE HERCULES: a fine bronze, signed Baccio Bandinetti, and dated 1556—14 *in. high*
Exhibited at the New Gallery, Early Italian Art, 1894
From the Hamilton Palace Collection
Vide Illustration

562 AN EQUESTRIAN STATUETTE OF PRINCE LOUIS D'ORLEANS, armed cap à pie, by Frémiet—19 *in. high*—on wood base carved with panels of acanthus foliage

562A A PAIR OF SILVERED BRONZE STATUETTES, of Landsnecht soldiers, bearing a banner and sword—11½ *in. high*

BARBEDIENNE BRONZES.

563 A PAIR OF CANDLESTICKS, of classic design, on tripod feet, honeysuckle and mask ornament—10 *in. high*

564 A PAIR OF BRONZE LAMP STANDS, adapted for the electric light, on tripod claw feet, bamboo-pattern stem—60 *in. high*

565 A PAIR OF GILT AND SILVERED LAMP STANDS en suite

566 ANOTHER PAIR

567 A CANDELABRUM, of classic design—24 *in. high*

568 A PAIR OF TRIPOD LAMP STANDS, copper-gilt – 21 *in. high*

569 A PAIR OF CANDELABRA, vase-shaped bodies chased with laurels
and swallows in relief, slender necks, branches for four lights
—20¼ *in. high*

DECORATIVE OBJECTS.

570 A REPEATING CHIMING CLOCK, by James, of London, in ebony
case with **dome** top, mounted with vase and scroll ornaments
in metal-gilt—15 *in. high*

571 A CLOCK, by Bolton Smith, of Wigmore Street, in satin-wood case
inlaid with shell ornaments in stained woods—11 *in. high*

572 A CHIMING CLOCK, by Thomas Pace, of London, in mahogany
case with dome top, mounted with terminal figures and scrolls
in chased or-molu—21 *in. high*

573 A PAIR OF LOUIS XVI. OR-MOLU WALL LIGHTS, with branches
for three lights, formed at the back as flaming vases of
classical form, and ram's-head handles, festoons of fruit,
flowers and ribbons below; acanthus branches chased with
leaves, and surmounted by female heads bearing baskets of
fruit and flowers in the style of Gouthière

574 A CABINET, of box and pear woods, fall-down glazed front **and**
cupboards at the sides, fitted with three shelves, panels **of**
looking-glass above and below, balcony above and below, and
four fluted pear-wood legs beneath—60 *in. long*, 17¼ *in. deep*,
69 *in. high*

Made **by Messrs.** *Jackson and Graham*
Exhibited at the Paris Exhibition, 1889

575 THE COMPANION

576 AN UPRIGHT CABINET, of pear-wood, open shelf beneath supported by four fluted legs carved at **the** top with acanthus-
leaf ornaments, the upper portion consisting in three glazed
cupboards, moulded borders, fluted above, and carved with
festoons of drapery and tassels

Exhibited at **the** *Paris Exhibition*

577 A COPPER-GILT TABLE CLOCK—*circa* 1590–1600—architectural
case supported on four square-shaped columns with balustrade, and surmounted by twelve vase-shaped ornaments, in
the centre of this a small gallery surmounted again by a
steeple, scroll and ball ornaments; silver dials partly
enamelled, elaborate astronomical movement, four regulating
dials; the whole chased with acanthus-leaf ornaments on a
matted ground; the base embossed and chased with Cupids
supporting baskets of fruit and flowers on **a** groundwork of
strap and floral ornament— 17 *in.* high, **the base 11** *in.* by
9 *in.*— in brass-bound glass case

    From the Wooley Pryors Bank Collection

578 A TABLE CLOCK, of copper-gilt—*Augsburg, circa* 1630—the body
is architectural in design, supported at four corners by columns,
and surmounted by a sphere, balconies, pilasters, and open
steeple containing small silver statuettes; the silver dial is
engraved with astronomical movement, four smaller dials for
regulating, and dials at the side; the whole is most minutely
pierced and engraved with tulips and passion-flower ornament;
the base embossed and chased with emblematical groups
representing the four quarters of the globe, bearing the
inscriptions " Europa," " Asia," " Africa," and " America ".—
22½ *in.* high, *the base* 10¼ *in. square*—brass-bound glass case,
24 *in. high*

    From the Wooley Pryors Bank Collection

579 A MIRROR, the frame of russet steel, at the top is a seated figure
of Mars, on either side crouching figures of Cupids supporting
festoons of drapery, flaming urns by their sides; the sides of
the mirror formed as pillars, with lions' heads holding festoons
of fruit and flowers, and supported at the base with terminal
male figures, female mask and drapery below, griffins on either
side; the whole of the work is embossed and chased, and
further enriched with minute damascening in gold, at the top
is inlaid an oblong panel of matrix of amethyst, on a pear-
wood mount

    Exhibited at the New Gallery, Early Italian Art, **1894**

580 **A CABINET**, with fall-down front and surmounted by a pediment of architectural design; the whole is richly encrusted with damascened russet iron, further enriched with precious stones—*Milanese, circa* 1560—the decoration consisting of—

(1) The fall-down front. In the centre an upright plaque of russet steel, 10 in. by 9½ in., representing Mars and Cupid, buildings in the background, in rich border of sphinxes, Romanesque warriors, cherubs, and four cartouche-shaped shields, containing cabochons of lapis lazuli and jasper. The whole of the details of the armour, &c., are minutely damascened in gold. On either side of the centre panel are three russet iron plaques damascened with spirited interlaced arabesques. Outside again, are two oblong panels containing oval cartouches of Mars and Venus, of similar workmanship to the centre panel, and likewise enriched with cabochons of lapis lazuli, jasper and onyx. Below this, running the breadth and depth of the cabinet, are plaques of russet steel embossed in the centres with a figure of Diana, griffins, acanthus foliage and amorini. The woodwork inlaid with parallel lines of ivory, Corinthian columns inlaid with flutings in gold and silver, gilt capitals and bases at the corners.

(2) The sides of the cabinet decorated with upright plaques of damascened and embossed russet steel, 9½ in. by 9 in., of similar design to the centre panel.

(3) The pediment, containing in the centre a circular bronze medal. On either side small upright damascened steel plaques of Roman warriors. The whole of the top and sides of the pediment covered with pierced ironwork of interlaced strap design, damascened with scrolls and dotted ornaments in gold.

(4) The interior, containing ten drawers overlaid with plaques of parcel-gilt silver, elaborately embossed and chased with Mars, Venus, Ceres, recumbent figures, trophies of arms, arabesques, fruit, and inlaid with cabochons and plaques of lapis lazuli, jasper, topaz, sapphires, &c. The interior of the fall-down front similarly enriched with engraved silver-gilt and precious stones.

42½ in. *long*, 32½ in. *high*, 19 in. *deep*—on architectural ebonised stand with six feet, and containing a single drawer —36 in. *high*

From the Hamilton Palace Collection

From the Beckett Denison Collection

Exhibited at the New Gallery, Early Italian Art, 1891

Vide Illustration

581 A LARGE EBONISED SHOW CASE, with plate-glass front—5 ft. 10 in. *high*, 5 ft. 8 in. *wide*

End of Fourth Day's Sale.

Fifth Day's Sale.

———————

On SATURDAY, MARCH 12, 1898,

AT ONE O'CLOCK PRECISELY.

———————

PICTURES.

1 PORTRAIT OF HENRY VIII. WHEN A BOY, in red dress with slashed sleeves, holding a dagger
    On panel—25 *in.* by 19½ *in.*

2 PORTRAIT OF A SPANISH GENTLEMAN, in white dress embroidered with gold, white ruff, holding a sword in his left hand
    30 *in.* by 25 *in*

3 PORTRAIT OF MARGARET DE VALOIS, in black dress with yellow embroidered front, white ruff, jewelled head ornament, gold chain and jewels
    20 *in.* by 16½ *in.*

4 PORTRAIT OF ANNE BOLEYN, in black dress **with** gold chain ornaments, black and yellow head-dress, holding a carnation in her right hand, coat-of-arms on the right
    Inscribed ANNA LOSTA TRIA HENRICI CORNELII AGRIPPAE DELECTISSIMA CONJUX, ANNO 1524, ÆTATIS SUAE, 21
    On copper—6¾ *in.* by 5 *in.*

5 PORTRAIT OF PHILIPPA OF HAINAULT, in black embroidered dress with jewels
    On panel—25½ *in.* by 17 *in.*

UNKNOWN.

6 PORTRAIT OF FRANCISCUS PETRARCH, standing to the right behind a balustrade, in dark dress, red lined hood

> "There is an original 'Laura' and 'Petrarch,' very hideous, both. 'Petrarch' has not only the dress, but the features and air of an old woman; and 'Laura' looks by no means like a young one, or a pretty one."—Note from Lord Byron's account of his visit to the Manfrini Palace, 1817.

On panel—13½ in. by 12 in.

From the Manfrini Palace

From the Heugh Collection, 1878

Exhibited at the New Gallery, Early Italian Art, 1894

7 PORTRAIT OF BLANCHE, daughter of Henri IV., who married the King of Bohemia; in blue embroidered dress, white collar, fur cap

On panel—20 in. by 14 in.

From the Collection of Lord Stafford, 1885

PORTRAIT OF A GIRL, *temp* Charles I., in black dress with gold embroidery, white lace collar and red bows, putting on her gloves—*dated* 1638

41 in. by 32 in.

LUCAS CRANACH.

9 THE NEGRO STANDARD BEARER OF CHARLES V., in fluted steel armour, gilt and jewelled, with large red hat and white plumes, holding the standard in his right hand and a sword in his left—*the wing of a triptych*

On panel—53 in. by 15 in.

From the Heugh Collection, 1878

LUCAS CRANACH.

10 CONSULTATION OF AFRICAN WARRIORS

On panel—26½ in. by 27 in.

From the Sale of the Baron de Bodin in Paris

J. B. FRANCKS.

11 AN INTERIOR OF A PALACE, with numerous figures dancing and musicians

22 in. by 37½ in.

HOLBEIN (AFTER).

12 PORTRAIT OF LADY ABERGAVENNY. Joanna, daughter of Thomas Fife Alan, Earl of Arundel, authoress, married George Nevill, Lord Abergavenny; in red dress with yellow sleeves, white cap embroidered with initials, jewel necklace and waist-band, holding a flower

On panel—12¾ in. by 14¼ in.

HONTHORST.

13 PORTRAIT OF A LADY, in black dress with puffed sleeves, large white lace collar and ruff, red bow and hair ornament

On panel—27 in. by 22½ in.

From the Collection of Colonel A. Ridgway, 1886

F. C. JANET.

14 PORTRAIT OF MARIE DE BOURGOINE, in rich dress with gold embroidery, slashed sleeves, jewel at the neck, large hat ornamented with pearls—*dated* 1476

On panel—12½ in. by 10 in.

From the Bohn Collection

From the Collection of the Marquis of Hastings

C. JANSSEN.

15 PORTRAIT OF A LADY, in blue dress with brown scarf and white
sleeves, with pearl necklace, earrings and bracelets
29½ in. by 25½ in.
From the Shandon Collection

C. JANSSEN.

16 PORTRAIT OF A GENTLEMAN, in armour, with long hair, slightly
turned to the left; said **to** be a portrait of Montrose
The companion
29¼ in. by 25¼ in.
From the Shandon Collection

SCHOOL OF MEMLING.

17 ST. CATHERINE OF ALEXANDRIA, St. Barbara and St. John
presenting two Flemish ladies, castle and river in the background, and two coats-of-arms
On panel—37 in. by 20½ in.

MIERVELDT.

18 PORTRAIT OF MARGARITA OF AUSTRIA, Queen of Spain, in black
dress embroidered with gold, lace ruff, feathers and pearls in
her hair
On panel—26 in. by 20 in.

F. POURBUS.

19 PORTRAITS OF HENRI IV., SULLY AND MADAME HENRIETTE,
COMTESSE DE VERNEUIL, as market figures with fruit and
vegetables, a chateau in the background
54 in. by 41 in.
Purchased from Thijs at Brussels, 1818
From the Earl of Clancarty's Collection

ROESTRATEN.

20 A EWER AND BASIN, with cups and other ornaments, on a table
    42 in. by 31 in.

VANDYCK.

21 PORTRAIT OF ADRIAN STALBENT, with ruff, and cloak over the
    right shoulder—*painted in grisaille*
        9 in. by 6¾ in.
        From the Collection of Dr. Burton, Bishop of Ely, 1864

ZUCCHERO.

22 PORTRAIT OF LADY ARABELLA STUART, in white dress em-
    broidered with flowers and armillary spheres, large lace
    ruff, pearl necklace, bracelet and head ornament, a fan in her
    right hand
        44 in. by 40 in.
        From the Bohn Collection, 1885

ZUCCHERO.

23 PORTRAIT OF MARY TUDOR, in red dress with large sleeves with
    puffs, white embroidered undersleeves and ruff, pearl orna-
    ments, head slightly to the left
        On panel—18½ in. by 15 in.

ZUCCHERO.

24 PORTRAIT OF A YOUTH, in white slashed dress, turned to the
    right, with coat-of-arms, and inscribed ÆTATIS SUÆ 13,
    1575
        On panel—18 in. by 13½ in.
        From the Collection of W. W. Warren, Esq., 1886

FINIS.

London: Printed by WILLIAM CLOWES & SONS, Limited, Stamford Street
and Charing Cross.